英汉对照典藏本

中世纪英国民间谣曲集

罗宾汉

[英] 弗朗西斯·詹姆斯·恰尔德 编

陈才宇 译

浙江工商大学出版社

·杭州·

图书在版编目(CIP)数据

罗宾汉：英汉对照 / (英)弗朗西斯·詹姆斯·恰尔德编；陈才宇译. —杭州：浙江工商大学出版社，2018.7

ISBN 978-7-5178-2813-6

Ⅰ.①罗… Ⅱ.①弗… ②陈… Ⅲ.①英语—汉语—对照读物②民间故事—作品集—英国 Ⅳ.①H319.4:I

中国版本图书馆 CIP 数据核字(2018)第 151421 号

罗宾汉

[英]弗朗西斯·詹姆斯·恰尔德 编　　陈才宇 译

出 品 人	鲍观明
策划编辑	钟仲南
责任编辑	沈　娴
责任校对	王黎明
封面设计	未　氓
责任印制	包建辉
出版发行	浙江工商大学出版社
	(杭州市教工路 198 号　邮政编码 310012)
	(E-mail：zjgsupress@163.com)
	(网址：http://www.zjgsupress.com)
	电话：0571-88904980,88831806(传真)
排　　版	杭州朝曦图文设计有限公司
印　　刷	杭州恒力通印务有限公司
开　　本	880mm×1230mm　1/32
印　　张	7.75
字　　数	180 千
版 印 次	2018 年 7 月第 1 版　2018 年 7 月第 1 次印刷
书　　号	ISBN 978-7-5178-2813-6
定　　价	58.00 元

译　序

　　罗宾汉这个名字在英国家喻户晓,妇孺皆知。我国的读者通过各种媒介,包括各类的读物和影视,也已耳熟能详。但许多读者恐怕并不知道罗宾汉的故事最初是以民间谣曲的形式传唱的。此次出版民间谣曲集《罗宾汉》(*Robin Hood Ballads*),有利于我们了解此人的"历史真面目"。尽管民间文学存在变异,但这些朴实无华的民间作品毕竟更接近"原生态",与后来文人凭想象随意虚构的罗宾汉故事有着本质上的区别。

　　罗宾汉是个神箭手,相传他生活在狮心王理查一世(Richard Ⅰ,1157—1199)时期,因遭人陷害被贬为法外人。所谓"法外人",即不受法律保护的罪犯,人人可以见而诛之。为了生存,也为了伸张正义,罗宾汉进入舍伍德森林,做起了打家劫舍的强盗。他手下有勇士一百多位,个个骁勇善战。凡是为富不仁的经过那里,罗宾汉就吹响号角,指挥手下勇士拦住来者的去路,让对方留下买路钱。但遇见穷苦人或被凌辱的弱者,他又会义无反顾地拔刀相助。

　　有关罗宾汉的谣曲保留下来的约四十多首(不包括异文),每首叙述一个故事,具有各自的独立性。这些谣曲大致可归到"绿林聚义""仗义劫财""除暴安良""英雄末路"四方面内容。

　　绿林聚义:这一部分共有十余首谣曲,叙述罗宾汉如何招纳四方义士,壮大起义的队伍。参加首次起义的好汉只有几十

1

人,大多数是后来加入的。他们投身绿林的原因不尽相同:有的是杀了人遭官府追捕而入绿林避难的(见《勇敢的小贩与罗宾汉》),有的是不堪封建主的迫害自愿投奔来的(见《罗宾汉与小约翰》),有的是奉命缉捕罗宾汉反被后者的义气感化而入伙的(见《罗宾汉与补锅匠》),还有的是罗宾汉慕其名专程请来入伙的(见《罗宾汉与短袍修士》)。每一个新来者入伙以前总要与罗宾汉先比试一番武艺,结果总是罗宾汉认输。这种描写我们不必看得太认真。罗宾汉在敌人面前英勇无比,但在自己未来的伙伴面前宁可扮演"弱者"的角色,这正好表现他胸怀坦荡、礼贤下士的美德。

仗义劫财:这一部分有七八篇谣曲。罗宾汉不是那种只认钱不认人的强盗,他抢劫的对象仅限于两种人:地方官和牧师。在中世纪的英国,这两种人即世俗政权和教会的代表。罗宾汉抢劫这两种人,其社会意义一目了然。这里选译了四首,其中《罗宾汉与赫里福德主教》和《罗宾汉拦劫牧师》,针对的就是教会势力;《罗宾汉与屠夫》和《罗宾汉与金箭》这两篇其实是姊妹篇,歌谣中被打击的对象同为诺丁汉郡长,一个顽固而愚蠢的封建官吏。

除暴安良:这一部分有近十首谣曲。打击的对象与前面仗义劫财的谣曲相同。不同的是,仗义劫财主要出于经济目的,而除暴安良是更激烈的武装斗争。《罗宾汉与爱伦·代尔》叙述的是罗宾汉如何帮助爱伦夺回他的情人的故事。《罗宾汉救维尔·斯塔特利》叙述罗宾汉率领他的人马救回自己的绿林伙伴。《罗宾汉劫法场》描写罗宾汉如何解放三个死囚犯的故事。《罗宾汉与吉斯本的盖尔》叙述罗宾汉如何打败前来征讨绿林好汉的官兵的故事。后两篇都以诺丁汉郡长被杀结束,雷同的现象可用民间文学所固有的变异性来解释。

英雄末路:这一部分的谣曲只有四五首,叙述罗宾汉如何受狮心王理查一世招安并由此导致绿林义军的解体和自己的死亡的故事。罗宾汉决定接受国王招安后,与他共患难的绿林兄弟觉得前途未卜,便纷纷弃他而去。罗宾汉十分伤感,生了一场大病。一位被他的仇人收买的修女(一说是他的堂姐)为他做放血治疗。这修女刺开他的血管后就将他反锁在室内。罗宾汉就在这放血"治疗"中流光了身上的血,生命就此结束。

虽然罗宾汉的故事是用谣曲写出的,但我在翻译时还是情不自禁要联想到我国的名著《水浒传》。宋江领导的起义与罗宾汉及其绿林好汉的事迹,无论在聚义的多样性方面,还是在武装斗争的目的方面,都有相似性。最后的结局也都是受招安。不同的是,罗宾汉接受招安后,他昔日的伙伴都离开了他,自谋生路去了;宋江的兄弟却没有离开他,而是甘愿做屈死鬼。这里面有着文化和价值观方面的原因。我们中国人是讲求"义"的,这"义"发扬到极致时,可以超越原则。人家英国人没有"义"的束缚。正是这种文化与价值取向的差异,导致了农民起义军不同的命运。

我的翻译依据的是弗朗西斯·詹姆斯·恰尔德 (Francis James Child,1825—1896) 搜集整理的《英格兰与苏格兰民间谣曲》(*The English and Scottish Popular Ballads*)。这是一套规模宏大的英国民间谣曲集成,流传于英格兰和苏格兰的民间谣曲,几乎悉数收入其中。上面我说的有关罗宾汉谣曲的篇目,依据的就是恰尔德的集子。我从那里面选译十四首,按内容做了编排。开头加的"序曲",是我从一首题为《罗宾汉正传》(*A True Tale of Robin Hood*)的谣曲中摘译来的。

但愿我的译文对了解"原生态"的罗宾汉传奇故事有帮助。
期待贤明者的批评。

陈才宇

2018年3月18日于杭州寓所

CONTENTS/目录

Prelude   *2*   *3*   序 曲

Robin Hood
and Little John   *6*   *7*   罗宾汉与小约翰

The Bold Pedlar
and Robin Hood   *26*   *27*   勇敢的小贩与罗宾汉

Robin Hood
and the Curtal Friar   *34*   *35*   罗宾汉与短袍修士

Robin Hood
and the Tinker   *54*   *55*   罗宾汉与补锅匠

Robin Hood
and the Bishop of Hereford   *76*   *77*   罗宾汉与赫里福德主教

Robin Hood's Golden Prize   *86*   *87*   罗宾汉拦劫牧师

Robin Hood
and the Butcher   *98*   *99*   罗宾汉与屠夫

Robin Hood
and the Golden Arrow   *114*   *115*   罗宾汉与金箭

Robin Hood
and Allan a Dale   *130*   *131*   罗宾汉与爱伦·代尔

Robin Hood
Rescuing Will Stutely   *144*   *145*   罗宾汉救维尔•斯塔特利

Robin Hood
Rescuing Three Squires   *164*   *165*   罗宾汉劫法场

Robin Hood
and Guy of Gisborne   *178*   *179*   罗宾汉与吉斯本的盖尔

The King's Disguise and
Friendship with Robin Hood   *206*   *207*   罗宾汉受招安

Robin Hood's Death   *228*   *229*   罗宾汉之死

COMMENTS/注释   *238*

ROBIN HOOD

By Louis Rhead

路易斯·瑞德 绘

PRELUDE

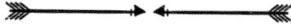

1

Both gentlemen, or yoemen bould,
   Or whatsoever you are,
To have a stately story tould,
   Attention now prepared.

2

It is a tale of Robin Hood,
   Which I to you will tell,
Which being rightly understood,
   I know will please you well.

3

This Robin, so much talked on,
   Was once a man of fame,
Instiled Earle of Huntington,
   Lord Robert Hood by name.

4

In courtship and magnificence,
   His carriage won him prayse,

序 曲

1

诸位乡绅，诸位自由民，

　五行八作各式人等，

今天讲的故事非同寻常，

　请大家这就留神静听。

2

故事说的是罗宾汉，

　下面我就给大家讲，

只要你把话儿听清，

　包你心情爽快非常。

3

这罗宾，有口皆碑，

　当年是个著名人物，

亨廷登伯爵是他的封号，

　人称罗伯特·汉勋爵。

4

他为人慷慨仗义，

　这方面没人能比；

And greater favour with his prince

  Than any in his dayes.

5

No archer living in his time

  With him might well compare;

He practisd all his youthful prime

  That exercise mort rare.

6

At last, by his profuse expense,

  He had consumd his wealth,

And being outlawd by his prince,

  In woods he livd by stealth.

7

The abbot of Saint Maries rich,

  To whom he mony ought,

His hatred to this earle was such

  That he his downefall wrought.

8

So being outlawed, as 't is told,

  He with a crew went forth

Of lust entter, stout and bold,

  And robbed in the North.

他爱品德高尚的人，
　　甚于爱全能的上帝。

5

同时代所有射手，
　　都难跟他比高强。
美好的青年时代，
　　全消磨在射箭上。

6

只因他过于慷慨大度，
　　最后财产开销罄尽；
国王贬他为法外人，
　　从此靠行劫为生。

7

圣母院院长家财万贯，
　　罗宾汉没给他送钱，
这人对此怀恨在心，
　　一手制造他的不幸。

8

罗宾汉成了法外人，
　　据传他带领随从进山，
那些人个个骁勇强悍，
　　从此剪径在北部英格兰。

ROBIN HOOD AND
LITTLE JOHN

➤━━━━━➤ ◄━━━━━◄

1

WHEN Robin Hood was about twenty years old,
  With a hey down down and a down
He happend to meet Little John,
A jolly brisk blade, right lit for the trade,
  For he was a lusty young man.

2

Tho he was calld Little, his limbs they were large,
  And his stature was seven foot high;
Where-ever he came, they quak'd at his name,
  For soon he would make them to fly.

3

How they came acquainted, I'll tell you in brief,
  If you will but listen a while;
For this very jest, amongst all the rest,
  I think it may cause you to smile.

4

Bold Robin Hood said to his jolly bowmen,

罗宾汉与小约翰[1]

1

罗宾汉当年双十年华，
　　浪里个浪，浪里个浪，
碰巧遇见那小约翰；
这棒小伙子性情开朗，
　　论剑术尤其内行。

2

虽名小约翰，却五大三粗，
　　个儿足有七英尺高，
他一来你会闻风丧胆，
　　打斗起来准得你先逃。

3

只要你肯劳神听一会儿，
　　我就谈谈他俩如何相见；
罗宾汉故事中这段趣闻，
　　你听后一定忍俊不禁。

4

罗宾汉嘱咐快活的弓箭手：

Pray tarry you here in this grove;

And see that you all observe well my call,

While thorough the forest I rove.

5

We have had no sport for these fourteen long days,

Therefore now abroad will I go;

Now should I be beat, and cannot retreat,

My horn I will presently blow.

6

Then did he shake hands with his merry men all,

And bid them at present good b'w'ye;

Then, as near a brook his journey he took,

A stranger he chaned to espy.

7

They happend to meet on a long narrow bridge,

And neither of them would give way;

Quoth bold Robin Hood, and sturdily stood,

I'll show you right Nottingham play.

8

With that from his quiver an arrow he drew,

A broad arrow with a goose-wing:

The stranger reply'd, I'll liquor thy hide,

"我想到森林里走走，
请大家在林地等候，
　这命令人人必须遵守。

5

"十四天来一直无事可干，
　因此我想出去逛逛；
如果被人打败回不来，
　那时会将号角儿吹响。"

6

他跟伙伴们一一握手，
　然后告辞他们上路；
不久来到一条小河边，
　碰见一位陌生男子。

7

他们巧遇在狭长的桥面上，
　两人谁也不愿意退让。
勇敢的罗宾摆开架势：
　"我要耍点把戏让你看看。"

8

说完他将手伸进箭袋，
　抽出一支鹅羽长箭，
陌生人说："只要你敢动一下弦，

If thou offerst to touch the string.

9

Quoth bold Robin Hood, Thou dost prate like an ass,
 For were I to bend but my bow,
I could send a dart quite thro thy proud heart,
 Before thou couldst strike me one blow.

10

"Thou talkst like a coward," the stranger reply'd;
 "Well armd with a long bow you stand,
To shoot at my breast, while I, I protest,
 Have nought but a staff in my hand."

11

"The name of a coward," quoth Robin, "I scorn,
 Wherefore my long bow I'll lay by;
And now, for thy sake, a staff will I take,
 The truth of thy manhood to try."

12

Then Robin Hood stept to a thicket of trees,
 And chose him a staff of ground-oak;
Now this being done, away he did run
 To the stranger, and merrily spoke:

我就把你往河水里揪。"

9

罗宾汉说:"你说话像头驴,
　　一旦我拉开这弓弦,
箭镞准穿透你傲慢的心,
　　那时你往哪儿把我揪!"

10

陌生人说:"你说话像个懦夫,
　　自己握弓瞄准我的胸膛,
而我却无武器防护,
　　手上只有这根哨棒。"

11

罗宾汉说:"懦夫之名我蔑视,
　　为此我要把弓搁置一旁,
与你一样也弄根哨棒,
　　看看到底谁是男子汉。"

12

罗宾汉走进灌木丛,
　　用橡木整制了一根哨棒,
然后跑回陌生人跟前,
　　和颜悦色对他说:

13

"Lo! see my staff, it is lusty and tough,

    Now here on the bridge we will play;

Whoever falls in, the other shall win

    The battel, and so we'll away."

14

"With all my whole heart," the stranger reply'd;

    "I scorn in the least to give out;"

This said, they fell to't without more dispute,

    And their staffs they did flourish about.

15

And first Robin he gave the stranger a bang,

    So hard that it made his bones ring:

The stranger he said, This must be repaid,

    I'll give you as good as you bring.

16

So long as I'm able to handle my staff,

    To die in your debt, friend, I scorn:

Then to it each goes, and followd their blows,

    As if they had been threshing of corn.

17

The stranger gave Robin a crack on the crown,

13

"你瞧,这哨棒多坚韧!
　　咱们这就去桥上比比武,
谁先掉进水里,谁就认输,
　　然后分手各自赶路。"

14

"我诚心照办,"陌生人说,
　　"谁逃跑就不是好汉。"
说完两人开始交手,
　　频频挥舞手中哨棒。

15

罗宾汉首先猛击陌生人,
　　打得他骨节咯咯作响;
陌生人说:"我要以牙还牙,
　　也给你点厉害尝尝。

16

"只要我挥得动哨棒,朋友,
　　就不屑负着债上天堂。"
两人你来我往不停抢打,
　　一如农夫摆弄打谷的连枷。

17

陌生人一棒从头上砸下,

Which caused the blood to appear;

The Robin, enrag'd, more fiercely engag'd,

And followd his blows more severe.

18

So thick and so fast did he lay it on him,

With a passionate fury and ire,

At every stroke, he made him to smoke,

As if he had been all on fire.

19

O then into fury the stranger he grew,

And gave him a damnable look,

And with it a blow that laid him full low,

And tumbld him into the brook.

20

"I prithee, good fellow, O where art thou now?"

The stranger, in laughter, he cry'd;

Quoth bold Robin Hood, Good faith, in the flood,

And floating along with the tide.

21

I needs must acknowledge thou art a brave soul;

With thee I'll no longer contend;

For needs must I say, thou hast got the day,

罗宾汉脸上顿时流血，
这使他恼怒到了极点，
　手中哨棒挥得更猛烈。

18

他已打得气冲牛斗，
　出手既神速又凶狠，
棒棒打得对手七窍生烟，
　好像他已烧成一团火。

19

陌生人也打得兴起，
　向罗宾汉投去狠狠一瞥。
随即向他腿上猛扫一棍，
　将他打落进溪水里。

20

陌生人放声哈哈大笑。
　"哟，好伙计，你在哪里？"
罗宾汉在急流中挣扎，
　一边诚恳地回答说：

21

"我知道你确实是位勇士。
　用不着继续比试下去，
我承认今天你是胜者，

Our battel shall be at an end.

22

Then unto the bank he did presently wade,
    And pulld himself ont by a thorn;
Which done, at the last, he blowd a loud blast
    Straitway on his fine bugle-horn.

23

The eccho of which through the vallies did fly,
    At which his stout bowmen appeard,
All cloathed in green, most gay to be seen;
    So up to their master they steerd.

24

"O what's the matter?" quoth William Stutely;
    "Good master, you are wet to the skin."
"No matter," quoth he; "the lad which you see,
    In fighting, hath tumbld me in."

25

"He shall not go scot-free," the others reply'd;
    So strait they were seizing him there,
To duck him likewise; but Robin Hood cries,
    He is a stout fellow, forbear.

咱们的打斗到此结束。"

22

罗宾汉很快游到岸边，
　　抓住一条树枝爬出水面。
然后提起心爱的号角，
　　吹出一阵嘹亮的声响。

23

号角声在山谷中回荡，
　　勇敢的弓箭手即刻到场。
人人披绿装，个个喜洋洋，
　　取道来到头领身旁。

24

"哟,出了什么事?"斯塔特利问,
　　"好头领,你浑身已湿透。"
"没什么,"他说,"眼前这汉子,
　　刚才把我打进水里。"

25

"别轻易放走他!"众人高呼,
　　他们想抓住他往水里按,
罗宾汉赶忙上前呵斥,
　　"住手,他可是条好汉!

26

"There's no one shall wrong thee, friend, be not afraid;

These bowmen upon me do wait;

There's threescore and nine; if thou wilt be mine,

Thou shalt have my livery strait.

27

"And other accoutrements fit for a man;

Speak up, jolly blade, never fear;

I'll teach you also the use of the bow,

To shoot at the fat fallow-deer."

28

"O here is my hand," the stranger reply'd,

"I'll serve you with all my whole heart;

My name is John Little, a man of good mettle;

Nere doubt me, for I'll play my part."

29

"His name shall be alterd," quoth William Stutely,

"And I will his godfather be;

Prepare then a feast, and none of the least,

For we will be merry," quoth he.

30

They presently fetehd in a brace of fat does,

26

"朋友,别怕,没人会伤害你,
    这些弓箭手都是我的助手,
总共六十九位,如你肯加入,
    马上就成他们的朋友。

27

"你穿什么服装合适?
    说吧,快活的浪人,别怕!
我还要教你张弓搭箭,
    将肥美的红鹿射杀。"

28

"咱们握握手吧,"陌生人说,
    "为你效劳我心甘情愿,
我约翰小个儿精力过人,
    相信我定能尽职尽心。"

29

"他的名字得改一改,"斯塔特利说,
    "这教父让我来担当,
大家快去准备酒宴,
    咱们要尽兴欢娱一场。"

30

大伙马上抬来两头肥鹿,

With humming strong liquor likewise;

They lovd what was good; so, in the greenwood,

   This pretty sweet babe they baptize.

31

He was, I must tell you, but seven foot high,

   And, may be, an ell in the waste;

A pretty sweet lad; much feasting they had;

   Bold Robin the christning grac'd,

32

With all his bowmen, which stood in a ring,

   And were of the Notti[n]gham breed;

Brave Stutely comes then, with seven yeomen,

   And did in this manner proceed.

33

"This infant was called John Little," quoth he,

   "Which name shall be changed anon;

The words we'll transpose, so where-ever he goes,

   His name shall be calld Little John."

34

They all with a shout made the elements ring,

   So soon as the office was ore;

To feasting they went, with true merriment,

还弄来冒泡的玉液琼浆，
　他们要给可爱的孩子命名，
　　绿林里办事讲究排场。

31

我得说他个儿足有七英尺，
　腰围也不下一厄尔，
大伙为这大个儿大摆宴席，
　罗宾汉亲自做感恩祈祷。

32

所有弓箭手站成一圈，
　他们都是诺丁汉的平民。
勇敢的斯塔特利与七名射手走上前，
　命名仪式举行得隆重庄严。

33

斯塔特利说："这孩子名叫约翰小个儿，
　这名字应该改一改，
前后两字颠倒一下吧，
　叫他小约翰[2]，无论上哪儿。"

34

命名仪式一结束，
　大伙打鼓击节沸反盈天，
欢天喜地进入筵席，

And tippld strong liquor gillore.

35

Then Robin he took the pretty sweet babe,
And cloathd him from top to the toe
In garments of green, most gay to be seen,
And gave him a curious long bow.

36

"Thou shalt be an archer as well as the best,
And range in the greenwood with us;
Where we'll not want gold nor silver, behold,
While bishops have ought in their purse.

37

"We live here like squires, or lords of renown,
Without ere a foot of free land;
We feast on good cheer, with wine, ale, and beer,
And evry thing at our command."

38

Then musick and dancing did finish the day;
At length, when the sun waxed low,
Then all the whole train the grove did refrain,
And unto their caves they did go.

将那玉液琼浆畅饮。

35

罗宾汉手拉可爱的小伙子，

　　将他全身上下打扮一番。

那一套绿衣最为中看，

　　此外还赠他大弓一张。

36

"你将成为最好的射手，

　　与我们一道在绿林漫游。

只要主教们的钱袋不空，

　　我们的开销就不犯愁。

37

"我们生活得像王公贵族，

　　虽然没有土地属于自己，

却吃上等乳酪，喝天下美酒，

　　要什么东西有什么东西。"

38

这天就在歌舞中度过，

　　最后夕阳变得朦胧；

绿林好汉隐入丛林，

　　回到自己居住的山洞。

39

And so ever after, as long as he livd,

Altho he was proper and tall,

Yet nevertheless, the truth to express,

Still Little John they did him call.

39

从那以后,只要他活着,

　尽管身材高大伟岸,

跟你说句实话吧,

　人们仍管他叫小约翰。

THE BOLD PEDLAR AND
ROBIN HOOD

1

THERE chanced to be a pedlar bold,

A pedlar bold he chanced to be;

He rolled his pack all on his back,

And he came tripping oer the lee.

Down a down a down a down,

Down a down a down

2

By chance he met two troublesome blades,

Two troublesome blades they chanced to be;

The one of them was bold Robin Hood,

And the other was Little John so free.

3

"O pedlar, pedlar, what is in thy pack?

Come speedilie and tell to me:"

"I've several suits of the gay green silks,

And silken bow-strings two or three."

勇敢的小贩
与罗宾汉

1

有位胆大的小贩，

　　有位小贩十分大胆，

他肩上扛着个包裹，

　　轻快地走在田野上。

　　　嘿哟嘿哟嘿哟喂，

　　　嘿哟嘿哟喂！

2

他碰上两个爱惹麻烦的浪子，

　　两个浪子专爱惹麻烦。

其中一个叫勇敢的罗宾汉，

　　另一个叫逍遥的小约翰。

3

"呔!小贩,包裹里有何物？

　　快快过来如实申明!"

"有几套翠绿绸衣,先生,

　　此外还有弓弦三五根。"

4

"If you have several suits of the gay green silk,

And silken bow-strings two or three,

Then it's by my body," cries Little John,

"One half your pack shall belong to me."

5

"O nay, o nay", says the pedlar bold,

"O nay, o nay, that never can be;

For there's never a man from fair Nottingham

Can take one half my pack from me."

6

Then the pedlar he pulled off his pack,

And put it a little below his knee,

Sying, If you do move me one perch from this,

My pack and all shall gang with thee.

7

Then Little John he drew his sword,

The pedlar by his pack did stand;

They fought until they both did sweat,

Till he cried, Pedlar, pray hold your hand!

8

Then Robin Hood he was standing by,

4

"如果你有几套翠绿绸衣,

　　此外还有弓弦三五根,

凭我这血肉之躯做证,"小约翰说,

　　"那东西咱们得平分。"

5

"这可使不得,"勇敢的小贩说,

　　"我决不答应你的要求,

从来没有一个诺丁汉人,

　　能从我这里将一半货物取走。"

6

小贩说完卸下包裹,

　　把它放在自己脚前:

"如果你能移动它一杆路,

　　整包东西就归你所有。"

7

小约翰抽出他的宝剑,

　　小贩等候在自己包裹边;

两人打得大汗淋漓,

　　直到小约翰告饶叫停。

8

罗宾汉坐在一旁观战,

And he did laugh most heartilie;

Saying, I could find a man, of a smaller scale,

Could thrash the pedlar and also thee.

9

"Go you try, master," sayd Little John,

"Go you try, master, most speedilie,

Or by my body," says Little John,

"I am sure this night you will not know me."

10

Then Robin Hood he drew his sword,

And the pedlar by his pack did stand;

They fought till the blood in streams did flow,

Till he cried, Pedlar, pray hold your hand!

11

Pedlar, pedlar, what is thy name?

Come speedilie and tell to me:

"My name! my name I neer will tell,

Till both your names you have told to me."

12

"The one of us is bold Robin Hood,

And the other Little John so free:"

"Now," says the pedlar, "it lays to my good will,

情不自禁哈哈大笑；
他说:"看样子得找个矮个儿,
　　代替你对付这小贩。"

9

"你自己上去试试,"小约翰说,
　　"头领,你自己快去试试。"
"凭这血肉之躯做证,"小约翰说,
　　"今晚我就见不着你了。"

10

罗宾汉抽出他的宝剑,
　　小贩等候在自己包裹边。
他们打得血流满面,
　　直到罗宾汉告饶叫停。

11

"小贩,你叫什么名字?
　　快过来跟我说说。"
"我不想把名字告诉你,
　　除非你俩先告诉我。"

12

"我们一个是勇敢的罗宾汉,
　　另一个是逍遥的小约翰。"
"哟,这倒很合我的心意,

Whether my name I chuse to tell to thee.

13

"I am Gamble Gold of the gay green woods,
  And travelled far beyond the sea;
For killing a man in my father's land
  From my country I was forced to flee."

14

"If you are Gamble Gold of the gay green woods,
  And travelled far beyond the sea,
You are my mother's own sister's son;
  What nearer cousins then can we be?"

15

They sheathed their swords with friendly words,
  So merrilie they did agree;
THey went to a tavern, and there they dined,
  And bottles cracked most merrilie.

我的姓名马上就报上。

13

"我是快活林中的甘姆勃，
　　浪迹在遥远的大洋彼岸。
因为在父亲庄园杀了人，
　　被迫逃亡在异国他乡。"

14

"如果你是快活林的甘姆勃，
　　浪迹在遥远的大洋彼岸，
那你该是我姨妈的儿子，
　　咱俩不就是表亲兄弟？"

15

他们把剑插回剑鞘，
　　说说笑笑握手言欢；
三人一道进入餐馆，
　　酒杯碰得叮叮当当。

ROBIN HOOD AND
THE CURTAL FRIAR

1

IN summer time, when leaves grow green,
  And flowers are fresh and gay,
Robin Hood and his merry men
  Were disposed to play.

2

Then some would leap, and some would run,
  And some would use artillery:
"Which of you can a good bow draw,
  A good archer to be?

3

"Which of you can kill a buck?
  Or who can kill a do?
Or who can kill a hart of greece,
  Five hundred foot him fro?"

4

Will Scadlock he killd a buck,
  And Midge he killd a do,

罗宾汉与短袍修士

1

夏日的森林莽莽苍苍，

　　鲜艳的百花陶然开放，

罗宾汉与众壮士，

　　使枪弄棒比高强。

2

有的跳高，有的赛跑，

　　有的摆弄防身匕首，

"你们谁拉得开强弓，

　　做一名高明的射手？

3

"谁能射中一头公鹿？

　　谁能射中一头母鹿？

谁能在五百步以外，

　　射中一头肥壮的红鹿？"

4

斯盖洛射中一头公鹿，

　　莫契射中一头母鹿，

And Little John killd a hart of greece,

    Five hundred foot him fro.

5

"God's blessing on thy heart," said Robin Hood,

    "That hath [shot] such a shot for me;

I would ride my horse an hundred miles,

    To finde one could match with thee."

6

That causd Will Scadlock to laugh,

    He laughed full heartily:

"There lives a curtal frier in Fountains Abby

    Will beat both him and thee.

7

"That curtal frier in Fountains Abby

    Well can a strong bow draw;

He will beat you and your yeomen,

    Set them all on a row."

8

Robin Hood took a solemn oath,

    It was by Mary free,

That he would neither eat nor drink

    Till the frier he did see.

在距离五百步的地方

　　小约翰射中一头红鹿。

5

"你的箭术真棒，"罗宾汉说，

　　"我主庇护在你身旁，

我要骑马到百里之外，

　　找个人来跟你较量较量。"

6

斯盖洛听后哈哈大笑，

　　他笑得真够开怀：

"芳汀寺有位短袍修士，

　　能将你俩都打败。

7

"芳汀寺那位短袍修士，

　　善拉一手硬弓强弩，

能打败你和手下侍从，

　　让大伙全成他的俘虏。"

8

罗宾汉以圣母名义，

　　起了一个庄严的誓。

他决心会一会那修士，

　　否则宁可饿瘪肚子。

9

Robin Hood pnt on his harness good,
   And on his head a cap of steel,
Broad sword and buckler by his side,
   And they became him weel.

10

He took his bow into his hand,
   It was made of a trusty tree,
With a sheaf of arrows at his belt,
   To the Fountains Dale went he.

11

And comming unto Fountain[s] Dale,
   No further would he ride;
There was he aware of a curtal frier,
   Walking by the water-side.

12

The fryer had on a harniss good,
   And on his head a cap of steel,
Broad sword and buckler by his side,
   And they became him weel.

13

Robin Hood lighted off his horse,

9

罗宾汉顶盔贯甲，
　　头上戴钢盔一顶，
腰间挂宝剑与圆盾，
　　这身打扮真够齐整！

10

长弓一把提手中，
　　那弓用硬木制造。
腰带上系一袋箭，
　　取道前往芳汀山坳。

11

芳汀山坳很快到达，
　　他勒住马头不再前行，
一眼看见那短袍修士，
　　正徒步走在溪水边。

12

短袍修士顶盔贯甲，
　　头上戴钢盔一顶，
腰间挂宝剑与圆盾，
　　这身打扮真够齐整！

13

罗宾汉翻身下马，

And tied him to a thorn:
"Carry me over the water, thou curtal frier,
Or else thy life's forlorn."

14

The frier took Robin Hood on his back,
Deep water he did bestride,
And spake neither good word nor bad,
Till he came at the other side.

15

Lightly leapt Robin Hood off the friers back;
The frier said to him again,
Carry me over this water, fine fellow,
Or it shall breed thy pain.

16

Robin Hood took the frier on's back,
Deep water he did bestride,
And spake neither good word nor bad,
Till he came at the other side.

17

Lightly leapt the fryer off Robin Hoods back;
Robin Hood said to him again,
"Carry me over this water, thou curtal frier,

把它拴在树丛边，
"背我过河去，短袍修士，
否则就要你的命。"

14

那修士背起罗宾汉，
涉水渡过深深河湾。
口中没有半句怨言，
一口气背到河对岸。

15

罗宾汉从他背上一跃而下，
修士这才开始发话：
"把我背回去，好伙计，
否则就给你一顿好打。"

16

罗宾汉背起那修士，
涉水渡过深深河湾，
口中没有半句怨言，
一口气背到河对岸。

17

修士从他背上一跃而下，
罗宾汉重复那番话：
"把我背回去，短袍修士，

Or it shall breed thy pain.

18

The frier took Robin Hood on's back again,
  And stept up to the knee;
Till he came at the middle stream,
  Neither good nor bad spake he.

19

And coming to the middle stream,
  There he threw Robin in:
"And chuse thee, chuse thee, fine fellow,
  Whether thou wilt sink or swim."

20

Robin Hood swam to a bush of broom,
  The frier to a wicker wand;
Bold Robin Hood is gone to shore,
  And took his bow in hand.

21

One of his best arrows under his belt
  To the frier he let flye;
The curtal frier, with his steel buckler,
  He put that arrow by.

否则就给你一顿好打。"

18

修士再次背起罗宾汉，
　涉入没膝深的河湾。
口中始终一言不发，
　直到背进河中央。

19

修士背他到了河中央，
　一撒手把他摔进河里：
"见鬼去吧，好伙计，
　是死是活全凭你自己。"

20

罗宾汉游向一丛金雀花，
　修士抓住一根柳树杆。
勇敢的罗宾爬上岸，
　马上将弓箭拿在手上。

21

他从腰间抽出一支锐箭，
　让它向着修士飞去；
短袍修士用他的圆盾，
　将射来的箭挡开。

22

"Shoot on, shoot on, thon fine fellow,
　　Shoot on as thou hast begun;
If thou shoot here a summers day,
　　Thy mark I will not shun."

23

Robin Hood shot passing well,
　　Till his arrows all were gone;
They took their swords and steel bucklers,
　　And fought with might and maine;

24

From then oth'clock that day,
　　Till four ith' afternoon;
Then Robin Hood came to his knees
　　Of the frier to beg a boon.

25

"A boon, a boon, thou curtal frier,
　　I beg it on my knee;
Give me leave to set my horn to my mouth,
　　And to blow blasts three."

26

"That will I do," said the curtal frier,

22

"再射再射,好伙计,

　　像刚才那样射下去!

你即使射上一整天,

　　我这靶子决不躲避。"

23

罗宾汉不断射击,

　　直到把箭全部射光,

然后双方手持剑与盾,

　　使出浑身解数作战。

24

他们从上午十点开始,

　　一直打到下午四时,

罗宾汉向修士屈膝,

　　请他答应一个要求。

25

"恳求你,短袍修士,

　　我屈膝向你恳求;

允许我将号角放在嘴边,

　　连续将它吹响三遍。"

26

"我答应,"短袍修士说,

"Of thy blasts I have no doubt;
I hope thon'lt blow so passing well
Till both thy eyes fall out."

27

Robin Hood set his horn to his mouth,
He blew but blasts three;
Half a hundred yeomen, with bows bent,
Came raking over the lee.

28

"Whose men are these," said the frier,
"That come so hastily?"
"These men are mine," said Robin Hood;
"Frier, what is that to thee?"

29

"A boon, a boon," said the curtal frier,
"The like I gave to thee;
Give my leave to set my fist to my mouth,
And to whute whutes three."

30

"That will I do," said Robin Hood,
"Or else I were to blame;
Three whutes in a friers fist

"号角耍不了花招，
但愿你鼓足劲儿吹，
    吹得一对眼珠爆掉。"

27

罗宾汉将号角放到嘴边，
    连续将它吹响三遍。
五十名壮士携带弯弓，
    飞快越过对面草甸。

28

"他们是什么人？"修士问，
    "为何急急赶到这儿来？"
"他们是我的随从，"罗宾汉说，
    "修士，你是否觉得奇怪？"

29

"我也有个恳求，"短袍修士说，
    "与刚才你的恳求一样。
允许我把手指放到嘴边，
    连续吹响口哨三遍。"

30

"这事好办，"罗宾汉说，
    "否则我会被人非难；
听听修士吹口哨，

Would make me glad and fain."

31

The frier he set his fist to his mouth,
  And whuted whutes three;
Half a hundred good ban-dogs
  Came running the frier unto.

32

"Here's for every man of thine a dog,
  And I my self for thee:"
"Nay, by my faith," quoth Robin Hood,
  "Frier, that may not be."

33

Two dogs at once to Robin Hood did go,
  The one behind, the other before;
Robin Hoods mantle of Lincoln green
  Off from his back they tore.

34

And whether his men shot cast or west,
  Or they shot north or south,
The curtal dogs, so taught they were,
  They kept their arrows in their mouth.

真叫人大喜过望。"

31

修士将手指放到嘴边,
连续吹响口哨三遍。
只见五十只看家狗,
飞快跑到修士跟前。

32

"每只狗对付一个人,
我自己继续对付你。"
"哟,我担保,"罗宾汉说,
"修士,这不是好主意。"

33

两只狗向罗宾汉猛扑,
一只在前,一只在后,
他那件林肯绿披风,
被它们从身上叼走。

34

绿林好汉从四面八方,
瞄准狗将箭纷纷射出。
修士的狗训练有素,
箭全被它们用嘴噙住。

35

"Take up thy dogs," said Little John,
  "Frier, at my bidding be;"
"Whose man art thou," said the curtal frier,
  "Comes here to prate with me?"

36

"I am Little John, Robin Hoods man,
  Frier, I will not lie;
If thou take not up thy dogs soon,
  I'le take up them and thee."

37

Little John had a bow in his hand,
  He shot with might and main;
Soon half a score of the friers dogs
  Lay dead upon the plain.

38

"Hold thy hand, good fellow," said the crutal frier,
  "Thy master and I will agree;
And we will have new orders taken
  With all the haste that may be."

39

"If thou wilt forsake fair Fountains Dale,

35

"把狗叫住!"小约翰说,

　"修士,这是我的吩咐。"

"你是谁?"短袍修士问,

　"竟敢在我跟前噜苏!"

36

"我叫小约翰,罗宾汉的部下,

　修士,我从来不说假话;

如果你不把狗叫住,

　就将你连狗一同格杀。"

37

小约翰握弓在手,

　又准又狠射出箭,

转眼间十来只狗,

　射中后倒地毙命。

38

"住手,好伙计,"短袍修士说,

　"我会与你的头领言和,

新的命令即刻颁布,

　此事我们马上去做。"

39

"如果你肯放弃芳汀山坳,

And Fountains Abby free,

Every Sunday throughout the year,

A noble shall be thy fee.

40

"And every holy day throughout the year,

Changed shall thy garment be,

If thou wilt go to fair Nottingham,

And there remain with me."

41

This curtal frier had kept Fountains Dale

Seven long years or more;

There was neither knight, lord, nor earl

Could make him yield before.

离开这座美丽的寺院，
每年只要一到礼拜日，
　就可领取一诺贝银[3]。

40

"如果你肯前往诺丁汉，
　进入绿林与我为伍，
每年只要一到节日，
　就能换一套新衣服。"

41

短袍修士住在芳汀山坳，
　说来已有七个多年头，
过去从没有王公贵族，
　能迫使他称臣稽首。

ROBIN HOOD AND
THE TINKER

1

IN summer time, when leaves grow green,

Down a down a down

And birds sing on every tree,

Hey down a down a down

Robin Hood went to Nottingham,

Down a down a down

As fast as hee could dree.

Hey down a down a down

2

And as hee came to Nottingham

A Tinker he did meet,

And seeing him a lusty blade,

He did him kindly greet.

3

"Where dost thou live?" quoth Robin Hood,

"I pray thee now mee tell;

罗宾汉与补锅匠

1

夏日的山野莽莽苍苍，

　　莽莽苍苍啊苍苍莽莽！

鸟儿在每棵树上欢唱，

　　鸟儿在欢唱啊在欢唱！

罗宾汉前往诺丁汉，

　　浪里个浪，浪里个浪！

一路上走得真匆忙，

　　嘿，浪里个浪，浪里个浪！

2

罗宾汉来到诺丁汉，

　　碰巧遇见补锅匠。

他见这人身强力壮，

　　便友善地跟他攀谈。

3

"你家住哪里？"罗宾汉问，

　　"请你这就跟我谈谈。

Sad news I hear there is abroad,

I fear all is not well."

4

"What is that news?" the Tinker said;

"Tell mee without delay;

I am a tinker by my trade,

And do live at Banbura."

5

"As for the news," quoth Robin Hood,

"It is but as I hear;

Two tinkers they were set ith' stocks,

For drinking ale and bear."

6

"If that be all," the Tinker said,

"As I may say to you,

Your news it is not worth a fart,

Since that they all bee true."

7

"For drinking of good ale and bear,

You wil not lose your part:"

"No, by my faith," quoth Robin Hood,

"I love it with all my heart."

听说外面消息不妙，
　　恐怕事情有些反常。"

4

"出了什么事？"补锅匠问，
　　"请你马上说给我听听，
我做的是补锅的营生，
　　居住在邦巴拉村。"

5

"这件事，"罗宾汉回答，
　　"只有我一人听说。
两个补锅匠被上了镣铐，
　　原因是他们喝酒胡闹。"

6

"如果就这点事，"补锅匠说，
　　"那我可要对你说，
你的消息一文不值，
　　尽管它千真万确。"

7

"麦酒、啤酒可口甘美，
　　不会让你丢掉脑袋！"
"不错，说句实话，"罗宾汉说，
　　"那东西我自己也酷爱。"

8

"What news abroad?" quoth Robin Hood;
    "Tell mee what thou dost hear;
Being thou goest from town to town,
    Some news thou need not fear."

9

"All the news," the Tinker said,
    "I hear, it is for good;
It is to seek a bolk outlaw,
    Which they call Robin Hood.

10

"I have a warrant from the king,
    To take him where I can;
If you can tell me where hee is,
    I will make you a man.

11

"The king will give a hundred pound
    That hee could but him see;
And if wee can but now him get,
    It will serve you and mee."

12

"Let me see that warrant," said Robin Hood;

8

"那你听见了什么消息?"罗宾汉问,
　"请把听见的跟我谈谈;
你穿街走巷云游四方,
　用不着凡事提心吊胆。"

9

"我听到这消息,"补锅匠说,
　"说起来倒有利可图:
有个叫罗宾汉的法外人,
　正遭到政府追捕。

10

"我带着份国王的逮捕令,
　可以随时拿他归案。
如果你知道他在哪里,
　事情还要请你帮忙。

11

"不管是谁只要找到他,
　国王就嘉奖一百英镑。
如果现在就把他抓来,
　这钱就进了你我的腰囊。"

12

"让我看看逮捕令,"罗宾汉说,

"I'le see if it bee right;

And I will do the best I can

   For to take him this night."

13

"That will I not," the Tinker said;

   "None with it I will trust;

And where hee is if you'l not tell,

   Take him by force I must."

14

But Robin Hood perceiving well

   How then the game would go,

"If you will go to Nottinghum,

   Wee shall find him I know."

15

The Tinker had a crab-tree staff,

   Which was both good and strong;

Robin hee had a good strong blade,

   So they went both along.

16

And when they came to Nottingham,

   There they both tooke one inn;

And they calld for ale and wine,

"是真是假应先弄清楚；

这件事我一定全力以赴，

今晚就可把他逮住。"

13

"这可不行，"补锅匠说，

"对任何人我都不轻信，

即使你不说他在那里，

我仍要让他束手就擒。"

14

那罗宾汉何等乖巧，

知道如何耍弄花招；

"如果你去一趟诺丁汉，

咱们就能把他找到。"

15

补锅匠带上楂木哨棒，

那哨棒结实而沉重；

罗宾汉腰挂一口宝剑，

两人一道赶路匆匆。

16

他俩来到诺丁汉，

一道进入一家酒店，

要了麦酒与啤酒，

To drink it was no sin.

17

But ale and wine they drank so fast
That the Tinker hee forgot
What thing he was about to do;
It fell so to his lot

18

That while the Tinker feel asleep,
Hee made then huste away,
And left the Tinker in the lurch,
For the great shot to pay.

19

But when the Tinker wakened,
And saw that he was gone,
He calld then even for his host,
And thus hee made his moan.

20

"I had a warrant from the king,
Which might have done me good,
That is to take a bold ontlaw,
Some call him Robin Hood.

尽情地开怀畅饮。

17

两人频频举杯喝酒，
　　补锅匠将自己的使命，
一股脑儿忘了干净，
　　这使罗宾汉有机可乘。

18

补锅匠呼呼在睡觉，
　　他趁机迅速离开酒店，
留下醉醺醺的补锅匠，
　　去付清巨额酒钱。

19

补锅匠酒后清醒，
　　发现罗宾汉不在身边，
便找到店主人那里，
　　向他如此诉苦抱怨：

20

"我有份国王的逮捕令，
　　这文件对我大有用场，
要逮捕一个法外人，
　　人们管他叫罗宾汉。

21

"But now my warrant and mony's gone,
  Nothing I have to pay;
And he that promisd to be my friend,
  He is gone and fled away."

22

"That friend you tell on," said the host,
  "They call him Robin Hood;
And when that first hee met with you,
  He ment you little good."

23

Had I known it had been hee,
  When that I had him here,
Th' one of us should have tri'd our strength
  Which should have paid full dear.

24

"In the mean time I must away;
  No longer here I'le bide;
But I will go and seek him out,
  What ever do me betide.

25

"But one thing I would gladly know,

21

"如今丢了逮捕令与银钱，
　　弄得这酒账无法付清；
刚才那人自称我的朋友
　　现在他已逃逸不见。"

22

"你的那位朋友，"店主说，
　　"就是人们所说的罗宾汉。
当他初次碰见你，
　　就把你戏弄了一番。"

23

"如果我刚才就知道，
　　同来的人就是罗宾汉，
那我们就该一展勇力，
　　看看谁的下场更惨。

24

"我现在得马上出发，
　　时间不容再消磨；
不管发生什么事，
　　一定要把他找到。

25

"剩下一事我乐意弄清，

What here I have to pay;"
"Ten shillings just," then said the host;
"I'le pay without delay."

26

"Or elce take here my working-bag,
And my good hammer too;
And if that I light but on the knave,
I will then soon pay you."

27

"The onely way," then said the host,
"And not to stand in fear,
Is to seek him among the parks,
Killing of the kings deer."

28

The Tinker hee then went with speed,
And made then no delay,
Till he had found then Robin Hood,
That they might have a fray.

29

At last hee spy'd him in a park,
Hunting then of the deer;
"What knave is that," quoth Robin Hood,

这里欠的钱共有多少?"
"只有十先令,"店主说,
　"这钱我决不会赖掉。

26

"要么让我将这提包,
　连同榔头暂作抵押。
等我找到那个无赖,
　回头再付你全部现金。"

27

"不必站着发急,"店主说,
　"找到他只有一条路,
你可以前去皇家猎园,
　他准在那里捕杀红鹿。"

28

补锅匠没有再耽误,
　他风风火火把路赶,
决心找到那罗宾汉,
　与他好好较量较量。

29

他终于在一片树林里,
　看见罗宾汉在捕鹿。
"哪来的毛贼,"罗宾汉问,

"That doth come mee so near?"

30

"No knave, no knave," the Tinker said,

    "And that you soon shall know;

Whether of us hath done most wrong,

    My crab-tree staff shall show."

31

Then Robin drew his gallant blade,

    Made then of trusty steel;

But the Tinker laid on him so fast

    That he made Robin reel.

32

Then Robing anger did arise;

    He fought full manfully,

Vntil hee had made the Tinker

    Almost then fit to fly.

33

With that they had a bout again,

    They ply'd their weapons fast;

The Tinker threshed his bones so sore

    He made him yeeld at last.

"胆敢挡住我的去路?"

30

"我不是毛贼,"补锅匠说,
  "这一点你马上就清楚。
咱们到底谁作恶多端,
  让楂木哨棒告诉你。"

31

罗宾汉抽出锋利的剑,
  那剑由优质的钢材炼成;
补锅匠出手极其迅速,
  打得罗宾汉天旋地转。

32

罗宾汉不由得心头火起,
  奋不顾身与他酣斗,
直打得那补锅匠,
  差点打算保命逃走。

33

两个人又打了一个回合,
  各自的武器频频挥舞,
补锅匠打得他筋骨发痛,
  终于使他支持不住。

34

"A boon, a boon," Robin hee cryes,

"If thou wilt grant it mee;"

"Before I do it," the Tinker said,

"I'le hang thee on this tree."

35

But the Tinker looking him about,

Robin his horn did blow;

Then came unto him Little John,

And William Scadlock too.

36

"What is the matter," quoth Little John,

"You sit in th' high way side?"

"Here is a Tinker that stands by,

That hath paid well my hide."

37

"That Tinker," then said Little Johhn,

"Fain that blade I would see,

And I would try what I could do,

If hee' l do as much for mee."

34

"我有个请求，"罗宾汉叫道，
　　"不知你能不能同意。"
"要我同意可以，"补锅匠说，
　　"但得先将你在树上绞死。"

35

补锅匠眼朝周围看了看，
　　罗宾汉乘机吹响号角。
小约翰即刻来到跟前，
　　另外还有威廉·斯盖洛。

36

"怎么回事，头领?"小约翰问，
　　"你为何蹲在路旁?"
"这里站着补锅匠，
　　赏了我一顿棍棒。"

37

"好一个补锅匠!"小约翰说，
　　"我倒要会会这混蛋，
试试自己有多大能耐，
　　看看他能把我怎样?"

38

But Robin hee then wishd them both
   They should the quarrel cease,
"That henceforth wee may bee as one,
   And ever live in peace.

39

"And for the jovial Tinker's part,
   A hundred pound I'le give,
In th' year to maintain him on,
   As long as he doth live.

40

"In manhood hee is a mettle man,
   And a mettle man by trade;
I never thought that any man
   Should have made me so fraid.

41

"And if hee will bee one of us,
   Wee will take all one fare,
And whatsoever wee do get,
   He shall have his full share."

38

罗宾汉倒有个好主意，

　　他希望两人停止争吵：

"从今往后我们同舟共济，

　　安安心心在绿林落草。

39

"为了快活的补锅匠，

　　我每年拿出一百英镑，

只要他活在这世上，

　　这钱就是生活的保障。

40

"这补锅匠勇敢非凡，

　　是个响当当的男子汉，

我罗宾汉从来没想到，

　　有人能使我如此惊惶。

41

"如果他愿意投身绿林，

　　我们就同富贵共患难，

不管得到什么东西，

　　他都能与大家一道分享。"

42

So the Tinker was content

With them to go along,

And with them a part to take,

And so I end my song.

42

补锅匠觉得很满意，
　愿意跟他们在一起，
从此他就是其中一员，
　我的歌也就唱到这里。

ROBIN HOOD AND
THE BISHOP OF HEREFORD

1

SOME they will talk of bold Robin Hood,
  And some of barons bold,
Bat I'll tell you how he servd the Bishop of Hereford,
  When he robbd him of his gold.

2

As it befel in merry Barnsdale,
  And under the green-wood tree,
The Bishop of Hereford was to come by,
  With all his company.

3

"Come, kill a venson," said bold Robin Hood,
  "Come, kill me a good fat deer;
The Bishop of Hereford is to dine with me to-day,
  And he shall pay well for his cheer.

4

"We'll kill a fat venson," said bold Robin Hood,
  "And dress it by the highway-side;

罗宾汉与
赫里福德主教

➤➤➤━━━━➤ ◄━━━━◄◄◄

1

罗宾汉早有人称颂，

　　贵族们也有人赞美，

今天单表赫里福德主教，

　　遭劫后如何受罗宾款待。

2

事情发生在巴恩斯代尔[4]，

　　发生在一片绿林中，

赫里福德主教来到那里，

　　身边跟着一班侍从。

3

"伙计们,杀一头鹿,"罗宾汉说,

　　"杀一头又肥又美的鹿;

赫里福德主教要来共餐,

　　那饭钱他将付得最足。

4

"杀一头又肥又美的鹿,

　　抬它到大路边燂毛,

And we will watch the Bishop narrowly,

    Lest some other way he should ride."

5

Robin Hood dressd himself in shepherd's attire,

    With six of his men also;

And, when the Bishop of Hereford came by,

    They about the fire did go.

6

"O what is the matter?" then said the Bishop,

    "Or for whom do you make this a-do?

Or why do you kill the king's venson,

    When your company is so few?"

7

"We are shepherds," said bold Robin Hood,

    "And we keep sheep all the year,

And we are disposed to be merry this day,

    And to kill of the king's fat deer."

8

"You are brave fellows!" said the Bishop,

    "And the king of your doings shall know;

Therefore make haste and come along with me,

    For before the king you shall go."

以便看住主教大人，
　　别让他从岔路走掉。"

5

罗宾汉与手下六位好汉，
　　一律打扮成牧羊人模样。
赫里福德主教来到那里，
　　见他们正围着篝火狂欢。

6

"哟，这是怎么回事？"主教问，
　　"你们为何如此喧哗？
一共只有这么几个人，
　　为何将国王的红鹿滥杀？"

7

"我们是牧羊人，"罗宾汉说，
　　"长年累月把牛群看管，
今天有心要快活一场，
　　杀一头国王的红鹿尝尝。"

8

"大胆的家伙！"主教说，
　　"这事一定会上报国王。
快准备跟我走一趟吧，
　　去国王跟前接受审判。"

9

"O pardon, O pardon," said bold Robin Hood,
    "O pardon, I thee pray!
For it becomes not your lordship's coat
    To take so many lives away."

10

"No pardon, no pardon," says the Bishop,
    "No pardon I thee owe;
Therefore make haste, and come along with me,
    For before the king you shall go."

11

Then Robin set his back against a tree,
    And his foot against a thorn,
And from underneath his shephetd's coat
    He pulld out a bugle-horn.

12

He put the little end to his mouth,
    And a loud blast did he blow,
Till threescore and ten of bold Robin's men
    Came running all on a row;

13

All making obeysance to bold Robin Hood;

9

"饶了我们吧,"罗宾汉说,
　"请求您饶恕我们,
将这么多人带在身边,
　有损您高贵的身份。"

10

"我不饶恕,"主教说,
　"对你们我不能饶恕,
快准备跟我走一趟,
　当面见见我们的君主。"

11

罗宾汉背靠在一棵树上,
　脚踩住一丛灌木,
从那羊倌穿的外套里,
　掏出小号角一只。

12

他把号角放到嘴边,
　吹出一阵嘹亮的声音。
七十个勇敢的壮士,
　列队跑到他跟前。

13

他们对罗宾汉十分恭敬,

'T was a comely sight for to see:

"What is the matter, master," said Little John,

　"That you blow so hastily?"

14

"O here is the Bishop of Hereford,

　And no pardon we shall have;"

"Cut off his head, master," said Little John,

　"And throw him into his grave."

15

"O pardon, O pardon," said the Bishop,

　"O pardon, I thee pray!

For if I had known it had been you,

　I'd have gone some other way."

16

"No pardon, no pardon," said Robin Hood,

　"No pardon I thee owe;

Therefore make haste and come along with me,

　For to merry Barnsdale you shall go."

17

Then Robin he took the Bishop by the hand,

　And led him to merry Barnsdale;

He made him to stay and sup with him that night,

那场面真叫人感动。
"头领,出了什么事?"小约翰问,
　"为何将号角吹得如此紧急?"

14

"这个赫里福德主教,
　对我们一点也不宽恕。"
"砍下他的脑袋,头领,"小约翰说,
　"将他的尸体丢进坟墓!"

15

"哟,饶了我吧,"主教说,
　"我请求你们饶恕,
如果早知道是你,
　我会走另一条路。"

16

"我不饶恕,"罗宾汉说,
　"对你我不能饶恕;
快准备跟我走一趟,
　去去巴恩斯代尔山谷。"

17

罗宾汉拽住主教的手,
　进入巴恩斯代尔丛林。
并要他晚上住在山上,

And to drink wine, beer, and ale.

18

"Call in the reckoning," said the Bishop,

   "For methinks it grows wondrous high:"

"Lend me your purse, Bishop," said Little John,

   "And I'll tell you bye and bye."

19

Then Little John took the bishop's cloak,

   And spread it upon the ground,

And out of the bishop's protmantua.

   He told three hundred pound.

20

"Here's money enough, master," said Little John,

   "And a comely sight't is to see;

It makes me in charity with the Bishop,

   Tho he heartily loveth not me."

21

Robin Hood took the Bishop by the hand,

   And he caused the music to play,

And he made the Bishop to dance in his boots,

   And glad he could so get away.

一道将各种美酒畅饮。

18

"叫人来结账吧，"主教说，
　　"我担心开销越来越大。"
"把钱袋借给我，主教，"小约翰说，
　　"然后就让你告辞回家。"

19

小约翰拿过主教的斗篷，
　　将他摊开在林地上，
并从他的旅行皮袋里，
　　搜出了三百英镑。

20

"钱倒不少，头领，"小约翰说，
　　"闪闪耀耀多么壮观，
我对主教倒产生怜悯，
　　虽然他并不讨人喜欢。"

21

罗宾汉牵住主教的手，
　　吩咐大伙将音乐弹奏。
他要主教穿着靴子跳舞，
　　然后才同意把他放走。

ROBIN HOOD'S
GOLDEN PRIZE

1

I HAVE heard talk of bold Robin Hood,
>   Derry derry down
>   And of brave Little John,
>   Of Fryer Tuck, and Will Scarlet,
>   Loxley, and Maid Marion,
>   Hey down derry derry down

2

But such a tale as this before
>   I think there was never none;
>   For Robin Hood disguised himself,
>   And to the wood is gone.

3

Like to a fryer, bold Robin Hood
>   Was accoutered in his array;
>   With hood, gown, beads and crucifix,
>   He past upon the way.

罗宾汉拦劫牧师

1

罗宾汉的故事我听过许多，

　　嘿，浪里个浪！

　　此外还有勇敢的小约翰、

特克修士、维尔·斯盖莱特、

　　劳克斯莱和少女玛丽安。

　　　嘿，浪里个浪，浪里个浪！

2

但今天要讲的这个故事，

　　恐怕能使你耳目一新，

故事说的是罗宾汉，

　　乔装打扮进入丛林。

3

罗宾汉装扮成修士，

　　头戴兜帽，身穿长袍，

脖颈挂念珠与十字架，

　　行走在林间大道。

4

He had not gone [past] miles two or three,

    But it was his chance to spy

Two lusty priests, clad all in black,

    Come riding gallantly.

5

"Benedicete," then said Robin Hood,

    "Some pitty on me take;

Cross you my hand with a silver groat,

    For Our dear Ladies sake.

6

"For I have been wandring all this day,

    And nothing could I get;

Not so much as one poor cup of drink,

    Nor bit of bread to eat."

7

"Now, by my holydame," the priests repli'd,

    "We never a peny have;

For we this morning have been robd,

    And could no mony save."

8

"I am much afraid," said bold Robin Hood,

4

他刚刚走出几里地，

　　便发现两位快活的牧师，

身上穿着黑色袍服，

　　骑着马翩翩而至。

5

"祝福你们，"罗宾汉说，

　　"怜悯怜悯我这穷修士，

请看在圣母的面上，

　　施舍我枚四便士银币。

6

"我来来回回走了一天，

　　什么东西都没得到；

既没一杯解渴的水酒，

　　也没一块充饥的面包。"

7

"凭圣母起誓，"牧师回答，

　　"我们身上一便士也没有；

今天上午遭人抢劫，

　　如今已一文不名。"

8

"我很担心，"勇敢的罗宾说，

"That you both do tell a lye;

And now before that you go hence,

I am resolvd to try."

9

When as the priests heard him say so,

Then they rode away amain;

But Robin Hood betook him to his heels,

And soon overtook them again.

10

Then Robin Hood laid hold of them both,

And pulld them down from their horse;

"O spare us, fryer!" the priests cry'd out,

"On us have some remorse!"

11

"You said you had no mony," quoth he,

"Wherefore, without delay,

We three will fall down on our knees,

And for mony we will pray."

12

The priests they could not him gainsay,

But down they kneeled with speed;

"Send us, O send us," then quoth they,

"你们两人准在说谎，
　　在你们离开以前，
　　　　我倒要搜查一番。"

9

　　两位牧师听到这里，
　　　急急忙忙骑马逃窜；
　　罗宾汉尽着脚力追击，
　　　很快把他们赶上。

10

　　罗宾汉抓住两位牧师，
　　　一齐从马背上拖下。
　　"饶了我们吧，修士，"牧师哀求，
　　　请你务必高抬贵手。"

11

　　"你们说身上没钱，"罗宾汉说，
　　　"那就马上想想法子。
　　让咱们跪下来祈祷吧，
　　　求主送钱到我们手里。"

12

　　两位牧师不敢拒绝，
　　　只得赶紧跪下祈祷：
　　"主啊，赐我们钱吧，"他们说，

"Some mony to serve our need."

13

The priests did pray with mournful chear,

Sometimes their hands did wring,

Sometimes they wept and cried aloud,

Whilst Robin did merrily sing.

14

When they had been praying an hours space,

The priests did still lament;

Then quoth bold Robin, Now let's see

What mony heaven hath us sent.

15

We will be sharers now all alike

Of the mony that we have;

And there is never a one of us

That his fellows shall deceive.

16

The priests their hands in their pockets put,

But mony would find none;

"We'l search our selves," said Robin Hood,

"Each other, one by one."

"赐钱满足我们的需要。"

13

牧师哭丧着脸祈祷，
　　时而将双手握紧，
时而高声地哀鸣，
　　而罗宾却唱得高兴。

14

他们祈祷了一个钟点，
　　两位牧师仍叹息不停，
罗宾这时要他们看看，
　　上帝送来了多少钱。

15

"凡是祈祷得到的钱，
　　我们大家都有份；
欺骗自己同伴的事，
　　这里绝不可以发生。"

16

牧师把手伸进衣兜，
　　老半天掏不出钱来。
"相互搜搜吧，"罗宾汉说，
　　"轮流搜搜每个人的钱袋。"

17

Then Robin Hood took pains to search them both,

And he found good store of gold;

Five hundred peeces preseutly

Vpon the grass was told.

18

"Here is a brave show," said Robin Hood,

"Such store of gold to see,

And you shall each one have a part,

Cause you prayed so heartily."

19

He gave them fifty pound a-peece,

And the rest for himself did keep;

The priests durst not speak one word,

But they sighed wondrous deep.

20

With that the priests rose up from their knees,

Thinking to have parted so;

"Nay, stay," said Robin Hood, "one thing more

I have to say ere you go."

21

"You shall be sworn," said bold Robin Hood,

17

罗宾汉经过仔细搜查，

　　发现他们带着许多金币。

总数不下五百英镑，

　　全部展示在林间草地。

18

"哟,这么多金币!"罗宾汉说,

　　"摊开来真让人开眼,

刚才大家祈祷很虔诚,

　　这些钱每人有一份。"

19

他们每人分得五十英镑,

　　其余的全归罗宾汉。

两位牧师没敢说二话,

　　唯有凄楚地悲叹。

20

两位牧师从地上爬起,

　　以为这下已走得成。

"且慢,"罗宾汉叫住他们,

　　"有一事还得说一声。"

21

"你们得发誓,"勇敢的罗宾说,

"Vpon this holy grass,

That you will never tell lies again,

Which way soever you pass.

22

"The second oath that you here must take,

All the days of your lives

You never shall tempt maids to sin,

Nor lye with other mens wives.

23

"The last oath you shall take, it is this,

Be charitable to the poor;

Say you have met with a holy fryer,

And I desire no more."

24

He set them upon their horses again,

And away then they did ride;

And hee returnd to the merry green-wood,

With great joy, mirth and pride.

"在这神圣的草地上。

从今后不管到哪里，

　都不可随便撒谎。

22

"你们得发第二个誓：

　在你们这一生中，

决不可引诱少女犯罪，

　更不可跟有夫之妇私通。

23

"你们还得发最后一个誓：

　对穷苦人要宽厚，

对行路修士要同情，

　这就是我全部要求。"

24

他这才让他们上马，

　允许他们继续赶道；

他则回转美丽的绿林，

　心中既高兴又自傲。

ROBIN HOOD AND
THE BUTCHER

1

COME, all you brave gallants, and listen a while,

With hey down, down, an a down

That are in the bowers within;

For of Robin Hood, that archer good,

A song I intend for to sing.

2

Upon a time it chancëd so

Bold Robin in forrest did spy

A jolly butcher, with a bonny fine mare,

With his flesh to the market did hye.

3

"Good morrow, good fellow," said jolly Robin,

"What food hast? tell unto me;

And thy trade to me tell, and where thou dost dwell,

For I like well thy company."

4

The butcher he answered jolly Robin:

罗宾汉与屠夫

1

来吧,勇敢的村民,

　　请大家过来费神细听,

　　嘿,浪个里浪,浪个里浪!

我想为你们唱一支歌,

　　唱唱非凡的弓箭手罗宾。

2

有一天,罗宾汉在丛林中,

　　碰上一位快活的屠夫。

他牵着一匹漂亮的马,

　　匆匆赶往市场卖肉。

3

"早安,好伙计,"快活的罗宾说,

　　"跟你做伴真叫人欢喜;

告诉我,你驮着什么东西?

　　做什么买卖?家住那里?"

4

屠夫回答快活的罗宾汉:

No matter where I dwell;

For a butcher I am, and to Nottingham

I am going, my flesh to sell.

5

"What is [the] price of thy flesh?" said jolly Robin,

"Come, tell it soon unto me;

And the price of thy mare, be she never so dear,

For a butcher fain would I be."

6

"The price of my flesh," the butcher repli'd,

"I soon will tell unto thee;

With my bonny mare, and they are not dear,

Four mark thou must give unto me."

7

"Four mark I will give thee," saith jolly Robin,

"Four mark it shall be thy fee;

Thy mony come count, and let me mount,

For a butcher I fain would be."

8

Now Robin he is to Nottingham gone,

His butcher's trade for to begin;

With good intent, to the sheriff he went,

"住哪里对我都一样，
我是个普通的屠夫，
　　这回为卖肉要上诺丁汉。"

5

"你的肉卖多少钱?"罗宾汉问，
　　"伙计，请把价格告诉我。
这可爱的马又卖多少?
　　做个屠夫我很高兴。"

6

"你问肉价吗?"屠夫回答，
　　"我这就如实告诉你，
连同这匹马，价格不贵，
　　只要付我四马克[5]银子就行!"

7

"给你四马克，"快活的罗宾说，
　　"另外再加四马克赏金，
你来点钱，我来骑马，
　　做个屠夫我很高兴。"

8

罗宾汉前往诺丁汉，
　　屠夫的生意从此开张。
他住进了一家客店，

And there he took up his inn.

9

When other butchers they opened their meat,

    Bold Robin he then begun;

But how for to sell he knew not well,

    For a butcher he was but young.

10

When other butchers no meat could sell,

    Robin got both gold and fee;

For he sold more meat for one peny

    Than others could do for three.

11

But when he sold his ment so fast,

    No butcher by him could thrive;

For he sold more meat for one peny

    Than others could do for five.

12

Which made the butchers of Nottingham

    To study as they did stand,

Saying, surely he was some prodigal,

    That had sold his father's land.

为了见到诺丁汉郡长。

9

别的屠夫已在卖肉，
　　罗宾汉才开始张罗。
他不知如何讨价还价，
　　作为屠夫他经验不多。

10

别的屠夫肉卖不出去，
　　罗宾汉很快换得现钱。
人家卖肉一斤只一斤，
　　他卖一斤要送两斤。

11

别的屠夫生意清淡，
　　罗宾汉已把肉卖光。
人家卖肉一两只一两，
　　他卖一两要送四两。

12

诺丁汉所有的屠夫，
　　站在那里犯嘀咕。
议论他是个败家子，
　　刚卖掉父亲的领地。

The butchers they stepped to jolly Robin,

    Acquainted with him for to be;

"Come, brother," one said, "we be all of one trade,

    Come, will you go dine with me?"

"Accurst of his heart," said jolly Robin,

    "That a butcher doth deny;

I will go with you, my brethren true,

    And as fast as I can hie."

But when to the sheriff's house they came,

    To dinner they hied apace,

And Robin he the man must be

    Before them all to say grace.

"Pray God bless us all," said jolly Robin,

    "And our meat within this place;

A cup of sack so good will nourish our blood,

    And so I do end my grace."

"Come fill us more wine," said jolly Robin,

13

他们来到快活的罗宾面前，

　　都想与他拉拉家常。

一个说："兄弟，咱俩是同行，

　　能否赏光先跟我去吃饭？"

14

"谁拒绝你，"快活的罗宾说，

　　"谁就该得到诅咒，

马上走吧，诚实的兄弟，

　　这里用不着再停留。"

15

他们来到郡长家里，

　　匆忙入席准备就餐；

又是这胆大的罗宾汉，

　　众人面前做感恩祭礼。

16

"主啊，赐福我们吧，"罗宾汉说，

　　"让我们将鱼肉吃够；

畅饮活血强身的美酒，

　　以上即我全部祈求。"

17

"来吧，把酒斟满！罗宾汉说，

"Let us merry be while we do stay;

For wine and good cheer, be it never so dear,

I vow I the reckning will pay."

18

"Come, brother[s], be merry," said jolly Robin,

"Let us drink, and never give ore;

For the shot I will pay, ere I go my way,

If it cost me five pounds and more."

19

"This is a mad blade," the butchers then said;

Saies the sheriff, He is some prodigal,

That some land has sold, for silver and gold,

And now he doth mean to spend all.

20

"Hast thou any horn-beasts," the sheriff repli'd,

"Good fellow, to sell unto me?"

"Yes, that I have, good Master Sheriff,

I have hundreds two or three.

21

"And a hundred aker of good free land,

If you please it to see;

And I'le make you as good assurance of it

"让我们在此尽兴寻欢,

美酒佳肴千载难逢,

　　所有开销记在我账上。"

18

"来吧,兄弟们尽情作乐!"罗宾汉说,

　　"让我们畅饮,杯子莫停;

临走前我会把账结清,

　　花它五百英镑也不要紧。"

19

"这人疯了,"屠夫们在议论。

　　"这人是个败家子,"郡长说。

"他一定刚卖掉自己的庄园,

　　这会又要把钱挥霍殆尽。"

20

"好伙计,你有牛羊吗?"郡长问,

　　"能不能把它们卖给我?"

"有,善良的郡长老爷,

　　我有二三百只牛羊。

21

"此外还有一百亩良田,

　　如果你乐意去看看,

我就全部转手给你,

As ever my father made me."

22

The sheriff he saddled a good palfrey,

   With three hundred pound in gold,

And away he went with bold Robin Hood,

   His horned beasts to behold.

23

Away then the sheriff and Robin did ride,

   To the forrest of merry Sherwood;

Then the sheriff did say, God bless us this day

   From a man they call Robin Hood!

24

But when that a little further they came,

   Bold Robin he chancëd to spy

A hundred head of good red deer,

   Come tripping the sheriff full nigh.

25

"How like you my hornd beasts, good Master Sheriff?

   They be fat and fair for to see;"

"I tell thee, good fellow, I would I were gone,

   For I like not thy company."

就像父亲转手给我那样。"

22

郡长给马套上鞍辔,

　　身带金币三百英镑,

然后与罗宾汉一道出发,

　　前去察看那些牛羊。

23

郡长与罗宾骑马而行,

　　不久来到舍伍德森林;

郡长说,"但愿天主保佑,

　　千万别碰上强盗罗宾!"

24

他们又往前走了一程,

　　勇敢的罗宾突然发现,

一百来只肥美的红鹿,

　　奔窜过郡长跟前。

25

"郡长老爷,这群牛羊如何?

　　它们一只只多么肥美!"

"好伙计,我不喜欢这群野兽,

　　否则就不会跟你来。"

26

Then Robin he set his horn to his mouth,

And blew but blasts three;

Then quickly anon there came Little John,

And all his company.

27

"What is your will?" then said Little John,

"Good master come tell it to me;"

"I have brought hither the sheriff of Nottingham,

This day to dine with thee."

28

"He is welcome to me," then said Little John,

"I hope he will honestly pay;

I know he has gold, if it be but well told,

Will serve us to drink a whole day."

29

Then Robin took his mantle from his back,

And laid it upon the ground,

And out of the sheriffe['s] portmantle

He told three hundred pound.

30

Then Robin he brought him thorow the wood,

26

罗宾汉将号角放到嘴边，
　　吹出三声嘹亮的音响。
小约翰率领众好汉，
　　很快来到他们跟前。

27

"您有什么吩咐?"小约翰问，
　　"好头领,请您告诉我。"
"我请来了诺丁汉郡长，
　　今天与大家一道进餐。"

28

"欢迎欢迎!"小约翰说，
　　"但愿他老老实实付饭钱，
我知道他身上带着金子，
　　会主动请我们吃上一天。"

29

罗宾汉从身上脱下披风，
　　随手把它摞在地上。
他从郡长的斗篷里，
　　搜出金币三百英镑。

30

然后罗宾汉带他走出森林，

And set him on his dapple gray:

"O have me commended to your wife at home;"

So Robin went laughing away.

让他骑那匹灰马回家。

"代我向尊夫人问候!"

说完,才大笑着与郡长分手。

ROBIN HOOD AND
THE GOLDEN ARROW

1

WHEN as the sheriff of Nottingham
Was come, with mickle grief,
He talkd no good of Robin Hood,
That strong and sturdy thief.
Fal lal dal de

2

So unto London-road he past,
His losses to unfold
To King Richard, who did regard
The tale that he had told.

3

"Why," quoth the king, "what shall I do?
Art thou not sheriff for me?
The law is in force, go take thy course
Of them that injure thee.

4

"Go get thee gone, and by thyself

罗宾汉与金箭

1

话说那诺丁汉郡长，
　　一路上唉声叹气，
口中诅咒着罗宾汉，
　　骂他是凶悍的盗贼。
　　　费喔咪喔嗒喔嘚。

2

这回他要去伦敦，
　　将遭劫一事上报国王。
以便理查一世君主，
　　对此事亲自管一管。

3

"你说我该怎么办?"国王说，
　　"难道你不是我的郡长?
法网恢恢,谁伤害你,
　　如何惩处全凭你自己。

4

"回去吧,动动脑筋,

Devise some tricking game

For to enthral you rebels all;

Go take thy course with them."

5

So away the sheriff he returnd:

And by the way he thought

Of the words of the king, and how the thing

To pass might well be brought.

6

For within his mind he imagined

That when such matches were,

Those outlaws stout, without [all] doubt,

Would be the bowmen there.

7

So an arrow with a golden head

And shaft of silver white,

Who won the day should bear away

For his own proper right.

8

Tidings came to brave Robin Hood,

Under the green-wood tree:

"Come prepare you then, my merry men,

安排一次射击比赛吧，
引诱所有反叛者参加，
　　如何惩处全凭你自己。"

5

郡长从伦敦返回，
　　一路上苦思冥想，
一边琢磨国王的话，
　　一边考虑将赛事筹办。

6

他自个儿揆情度理：
　　这场比赛一旦举行，
那班强悍的法外人，
　　定会前来比试射箭。

7

他于是铸造一支箭，
　　箭镞铸金，杆儿铸银。
谁在比赛那天取胜，
　　谁就获得这支宝箭。

8

消息很快传进绿林，
　　传给勇敢的罗宾汉。
"伙计们，大家准备一下，

We'll go you sport to see."

9

With that stept forth a brave young man,

    David of Doncaster:

"Master," said he, "be ruld by me,

    From the green-wood we'll not stir.

10

"To tell the truth, I'm well informed

    You match is a wile;

The sheriff, I wiss, devises this

    Us archers to beguile."

11

"O thou smells of a coward," said Robin Hood,

    "Thy words does not please me;

Come on't what will, I'll try my skill

    At you brave archery."

12

O then bespoke brave Little John:

    Come, let us thither gang;

Come listen to me, how it shall be

    That we need not be kend.

那场面值得去看看。"

9

这时走上唐克斯特的大卫，
　　一位勇敢的年轻人。
"头领，"他说，"依我之见，
　　我们不应该离开绿林。

10

"说真的，我已得到可靠情报，
　　那场比赛是一个阴谋，
郡长如此握筹布画，
　　是为了引我们上钩。"

11

"你像个胆小鬼，"罗宾汉说，
　　"你的话不称我的心；
不管将发生什么事，
　　我都要去比比射箭。"

12

小约翰这时出来说话：
　　"伙计们，快集合待命，
听我说，不管比赛如何进行，
　　都用不着我们担心。

13

Our mantles, all of Lincoln green,

    Behind us we will leave;

We'll dress us all so several

    They shall not us perceive.

14

One shall wear white, another red,

    One yellow, another blue:

Thus in disguise, to the exercise

    We'll gang, whateer ensue.

15

Forth from the green-wood they are gone,

    With hearts all firm and stout,

Resolving [then] with the sheriff's men

    To have a hearty bout.

16

So themselves they mixed with the rest,

    To prevent all suspicion;

For if they should together hold

    They thought [it] no discretion.

17

So the sheriff looking round about,

13

"我们那林肯绿披风，

　　全部留下不要穿去。

服装颜色要各不相同，

　　让他们无法把咱们认出。

14

"一人穿白，另一人就穿红，

　　一人穿黄，另一人就穿蓝。

大家乔装打扮去参赛，

　　发生什么事用不着管。"

15

他们个个心诚志坚，

　　乔装打扮出了绿林，

决心跟郡长手下的人，

　　比比谁更善于射箭。

16

为了提防别人怀疑，

　　他们分散混入人群。

如果需要集体行动，

　　人人都能绝对服从。

17

郡长面对八百观众，

Amongst eight hundred men,

But could not see the sight that he

Had long expected then.

18

Some said, If Robin Hood was here,

And all his men to boot,

Sure none of them could pass these men,

So bravely they do shoot.

19

"Ay," quoth the sheriff, and scratchd his head,

"I thought he would have been here;

I thought he would, but, tho he's bold,

He durst not now appear."

20

O that word grieved Robin Hood to the heart;

He vexëd in his blood;

Eer long, thought he, thou shalt well see

That here was Robin Hood.

21

Some cried, Blue jacket! another cried, Brown!

And the third cried, Brave Yellow!

But the fourth man said, Yon man in red

前前后后到处张望,
但始终没能如愿以偿,
　见到期待已久的景象。

18

有人说,如果罗宾在场,
　加上他手下那班好汉,
就无人能赢过他们,
　论射箭他们最强。

19

"嘿嘿,"郡长在搔头皮,
　"我猜他定在人群里,
不过,虽然他胆大包天,
　谅他不敢出场比试。"

20

这话刺痛了罗宾汉,
　恼得他热血沸腾。
"等着瞧,"他心里在说,
　"我罗宾会出场让你看看。"

21

观众欢呼:蓝衣胜了!灰衣胜了!
　再欢呼:勇敢的黄衣胜了!
又欢呼:红衣!红衣!红衣胜了!

In this place has no fellow.

22

For that was Robin Hood himself,
 For he was cloathd in red;
At every shot the prize he got,
 For he was both sure and dead.

23

So the arrow with the golden head
 And shaft of silver white
Brave Robin Hood won, and bore with him
 For his own proper right.

24

These outlaws there, that very day,
 To shun all kind of doubt,
By three or four, no less no more,
 As they went in came out.

25

Until they all assernbled were
 Under the green-wood shade,
Where they reports, in pleasant sport,
 What brave pastime they made

最后胜利属于红衣箭手。

22

其实那人就是罗宾汉，

　　那天他穿的正是红衣裳。

百发百中的神射手，

　　他箭无虚发拔头筹。

23

他赢得了那支宝箭，

　　箭镞铸金，杆儿铸银。

勇敢的罗宾把箭领走，

　　如今它已归他所有。

24

为了避免种种猜疑，

　　那天法外人像来时那样，

三个一群，两个一对，

　　分散地撤出赛场。

25

直到大家重新会合，

　　在那葱绿的树荫下，

人人兴致勃勃地谈论，

　　刚才那场勇敢的戏耍。

26

Says Robin Hood, All my care is,

How that yon sheriff may

Know certainly that it was I

That bore his arrow away.

27

Says Little John, My counsel good

Did take effect before,

So therefore now, if you'll allow,

I will advise once more.

28

"Speak on, speak on," said Robin Hood,

"Thy wit's both quick and sound;

[I know no man amongst us can

For wit like thee be found."]

29

"This I advise," said Little John;

"That a letter shall be pend,

And when it is done, to Nottingham

You to the sheriff shall send."

30

"That is well advised," said Robin Hood,

26

罗宾汉这时开口说话：

　"现有一事我最关心：

如何设法让郡长知道，

　是我赢得了他的金箭。"

27

"我的建议，"小约翰说，

　"先前每次你都采纳，

如果你允许，头领，

　让我再将建议奉告。"

28

"说吧，说吧，"罗宾汉说，

　"你的思维敏捷而超群，

我知道在咱们当中，

　再找不出你这样的人。"

29

"我建议，"小约翰说，

　"我建议修一封信函，

派人带进诺丁汉，

　交到那郡长手上。"

30

"主意倒不错，"罗宾汉说，

"But how must it be sent?"

"Pugh! when you please, it's done with ease,
　　Master, be you content.

31

"I'll stick it on my arrow's head,
　　And shoot it into the town;
The mark shall show where it must go
　　When ever it lights down."

32

The project it was full performd;
　　The sheriff that letter had;
Which when he read, he scratchd his head,
　　And rav'd like one that's mad.

33

So we'll leave him chafing in his grease,
　　Which will do him no good;
Now, my friends, attend, and hear the end
　　Of honest Robin Hood.

"但这函件如何交递?"

"咳,只要你高兴,这事不难,
　头领,我能办得让你满意。

31

"我要将它扎在箭镞上,
　然后将箭射进城里,
落地后该往哪里送,
　自有上面的标记表明。"

32

事情办得非常出色,
　郡长及时收到这封信。
他一边读,一边搔头皮,
　恼怒得差点乱了神经。

33

让他沮丧地嗷叫去吧,
　反正一切已无济于事。
朋友,请注意,罗宾的故事,
　今天就讲到这里。

ROBIN HOOD AND
ALLAN A DALE

1

COME listen to me, you gallants so free,
   All you that loves mirth for to hear,
And I will you tell of a bold outlaw,
   That lived in Nottinghamshire. (*bis.*)

2

As Robin Hood in the forrest stood,
   All under the green-wood tree,
There was he ware of a brave young man,
   As fine as fine might be.

3

The youngster was clothed in scarlet red,
   In scarlet fine and gay,
And he did frisk it over the plain,
   And chanted a roundelay.

4

As Robin Hood next morning stood,
   Amongst the leaves so gay,

罗宾汉与爱伦·代尔

1

来吧，勇敢的人们，
　　你们都爱听逸事趣闻，
今天我就讲一个法外人，
　　当年居住在诺丁汉郡。

2

我要讲的是罗宾汉，
　　那天他站在林荫下，
发现路上有个年轻人，
　　模样儿英俊而潇洒。

3

这人身穿大红礼服，
　　一身打扮赏心悦目。
礼服在路面上飘拂，
　　口中哼着一支回旋曲。

4

但是到了第二天上午，
　　罗宾汉在快活的树林里，

There did he espy the same young man
    Come drooping along the way.

5

The scarlet he wore the day before,
    It was clean cast away;
And every step he fetcht a sigh,
    "Alack and a well a day!"

6

Then stepped forth brave Little John,
    And Nick the millers son,
Which made the young man bend his bow,
    When as he see them come.

7

"Stand off, stand off," the young man said,
    "What is your will with me?"
"You must come before our master straight,
    Vnder yon green-wood tree."

8

And when he came bold Robin before,
    Robin askt him courteously,
O hast thou any money to spare
    For my merry men and me?

再次发现那个年轻人，
　　却见他一路上垂头丧气。

5

他头天穿的红礼服，
　　这回却没有披身上。
他走一步要叹息一下：
　　"哎呀，今天过得窝囊。"

6

勇敢的小约翰迎上前去，
　　磨坊主儿子尼克随后跟上。
年轻人看见有人过来，
　　张弓搭箭准备迎战。

7

"闪开！闪开！"年轻人说，
　　"你们想要我干啥？"
"请你见见我们头领，
　　他就在那边树下。"

8

他来到勇敢的罗宾跟前，
　　罗宾礼貌地向他问话。
"请问你身上是否有钱，
　　分点给我与我的部下？"

9

"I have no money," the yound man said,
　"But five shillings and a ring;
And that I have kept this seven long years,
　To have it at my wedding.

10

"Yesterday I should have married a maid,
　But she is now from me tane,
And chosen to be an old knights delight,
　Whereby my poor heart is slain."

11

"What is thy name?" then said Robin Hood,
　"Come tell me, without any fail:"
"By the faith of my body," then said the young man,
　"My name it is Allan a Dale."

12

"What wilt thou give me," said Robin Hood,
　"In ready gold or fee,
To help thee to thy true-love again,
　And deliver her unto thee?"

13

"I have no money," then quoth the young man,

9

"我没有钱,"年轻人说,

　"只有一枚戒指和五个先令,

这戒指我保存了七年,

　打算拿它作为结婚礼品。

10

"昨天我本该与一小姐成婚,

　今天她却成了别人的新娘。

有位老骑士将她占有,

　留下我只有失意怅惘。"

11

"你叫什么名字?"罗宾汉问,

　"不必迟疑,快告诉我。"

"凭这血肉之躯做证,"年轻人说,

　"我的名字叫爱伦·代尔。"

12

"如果我帮助你,"罗宾汉说,

　"让心上人回到你身边,

你准备拿什么报答我?

　是现成金币还是赏银?"

13

"我没有钱,"年轻人说,

"No ready gold nor fee,

But I will swear upon a book

Thy true servant for to be."

14

"How many miles is it to thy true-love?

Come tell me without any guile:"

"By the faith of my body," then said the young man,

"It is but five little mile."

15

Then Robin he hasted over the plain,

He did neither stint nor lin,

Vntil he came unto the church

Where Allan should keep his wedding.

16

"What dost thou do here?" the bishop he said,

"I prethee now tell to me:"

"I am a bold harper," quoth Robin Hood,

"And the best in the north countrey."

17

"O welcome, O welcome," the bishop he said,

"That musick best pleaseth me;"

"You shall have no musick," quoth Robin Hood,

"既没金币也没赏银,
我会凭着《圣经》起誓,
　做你的侍从赤胆忠心。"

14

"你心上人离此多少路?
　快告诉我,不必犹豫。"
"凭这血肉之躯做证,"年轻人说,
　"路程倒只有五英里。"

15

罗宾汉急急忙忙上路,
　途中一刻也不停,
一口气赶到教堂,
　婚礼将在那里举行。

16

"你想干什么?"主教问,
　"请你如实向我奉告。"
"我是个琴师,"罗宾汉说,
　"在北方我的琴弹得最好。"

17

"欢迎欢迎!"主教说,
　"音乐最能陶冶性情。"
"不见到新娘与新郎,"罗宾汉说,

"Till the bride and the bridegroom I see."

18

With that came in a wealthy knight,

Which was both grave and old,

And after him a finikin lass,

Did shine like glistering gold.

19

"This is no fit match," quoth bold Robin Hood,

"That you do seem to make here;

For since we are come unto the church,

The bride she shall chuse her own dear."

20

Then Robin Hood put his horn to his month,

And blew blasts two or three;

When four and twenty bowmen bold

Came leaping over the lee.

21

And when they came into the church-yard,

Marching all on a row,

The first man was Allan a Dale,

To give bold Robin his bow.

"我不会弹乐曲给你听。"

18

一位富有的骑士走进教堂，
　　这人老态龙钟表情沉重，
身后跟着娇弱的小姐，
　　模样金子般闪着光芒。

19

"这不相称，"罗宾汉说，
　　"你俩看上去不相称；
我们既然来到教堂，
　　该让新娘选择意中人。"

20

罗宾汉把号角放到嘴边，
　　吹出一阵阵嘹亮的声音；
二十四名勇敢的弓箭手，
　　疾步穿出前面草甸。

21

他们排成一列纵队，
　　迈步走进教堂大院。
爱伦·代尔就在其中，
　　他率先向罗宾汉致敬。

22

"This is thy true-love," Robin he said,

"Young Allan, as I hear say;

And you shall be married at this same time,

Before we depart away."

23

"That shall not be," the bishop he said,

"For thy word shall not stand;

They shall be three times askt in the church,

As the law is of our land."

24

Robin Hood pulld off the bishops coat,

And put it upon Little John;

"By the faith of my body," then Robin said,

"This cloath doth make thee a man."

25

When Little John went into the quire,

The people began for to laugh;

He askt them seven times in the church,

Least three times should not be enough.

26

"Who gives me this maid?" then said Little John;

22

“这才是你的意中人，”罗宾汉说，

　“听说年轻人的名字叫爱伦；

我们大伙撤离以前，

　你就与他结成良缘。”

23

“这可使不得，”主教说，

　“你的话不能算数，

我国法律明文规定，

　新人得由我连问三次。”

24

罗宾汉剥去主教的衣裳，

　将它披到小约翰身上。

“凭这血肉之躯做证，”罗宾汉说，

　“你穿上倒也仪表堂堂。”

25

小约翰走向唱诗班，

　人们乐得嘻嘻哈哈，

他连问新人七次，

　唯恐三次不到家。

26

“谁是少女的傧相？”小约翰问，

Quoth Robin, That do I,

And he that doth take her from Allan a Dale

Full dearly he shall her buy.

27

And thus laving ended this merry wedding,

The bride lookt as fresh as a queen,

And so they returnd to the merry green-wood,

Amongst the leaves so green.

"是我罗宾汉!"罗宾汉回答,
"我从爱伦·代尔那里带她来,
　他俩正好配对成双。"

27

欢乐的婚礼就此结束,
　新娘像皇后般娇艳,
众好汉返回自己的绿林,
　很快消失在翠色中间。

ROBIN HOOD RESCUING
WILL STUTELY

1

WHEN Robin Hood in the green-wood livd,

    Derry derry down

    Vnder the green-wood tree,

Tidings there came to him with speed,

    Tidings for certainty,

        Hey down derry derry down

2

That Will Stutely surprized was,

    And eke in prison lay;

Three varlets that the sheriff had hired

    Did likely him betray.

3

I, and to-morrow hanged must be,

    To-morrow as soon as it is day;

But before they could this victory get,

    Two of them did Stutely slay.

罗宾汉救
维尔·斯塔特利

1

罗宾汉生活在绿林，

　　嘿，浪个里浪！

　　罗宾汉生活在林间，

不幸的消息很快传来，

　　不幸的消息确凿可信。

　　　嘿,浪个里浪,浪个里浪！

2

消息说维尔·斯塔特利遭遇不测，

　　这会儿正关押在牢房。

三个歹徒被郡长收买，

　　是他们把维尔背叛。

3

哎呀,到明日天一亮,

　　他就要死在绞刑架下。

三个歹徒来不及庆功,

　　有两个已被维尔所杀。

4

When Robin Hood he heard this news,
    Lord! he was grieved sore,
I, and unto his merry men[said],
    Who altogether swore,

5

That Will Stutely should rescued be,
    And be brought safe again;
Or else should many a gallant wight
    For his sake there be slain.

6

He cloathed himself in scarlet then,
    His men were all in green;
A finer show, throughout the world,
    In no place could be seen.

7

Good lord! it was a gallant sight
    To see them all on a row;
With every man a good broad sword,
    And eke a good yew bow.

8

Forth of the green-wood are they gone,

4

罗宾汉听到这消息，

　哟，心里多么悲切！

他召集手下众壮士，

　一起庄严地发誓：

5

"一定要将维尔救出！

　一定要让他平安返回！

否则为了他的缘故，

　宁可更多英雄掉脑袋！"

6

罗宾汉穿一件猩红外氅，

　众壮士一律穿绿色衣裳，

比这更壮观的场面，

　四海之内再难一见。

7

哟，他们排成一列横队，

　那场面看上去真够气派，

人人身上佩一把宝剑，

　还有紫杉弯弓随身带。

8

他们个个英勇绝伦，

Yea, all couragiously,

Resolving to bring Stutely home,

Or every man to die.

9

And when they came the castle neer

Whereas Will Stutely lay,

"I hold it good," saith Robin Hood,

"Wee here in ambush stay,

10

"And send one forth some news to hear,

To yonder palmer fair,

That stands under the castle-wall;

Some news he may declare."

11

With that steps forth a brave yound man,

Which was of courage bold;

Thus hee did say to the old man:

I pray thee, palmer old,

12

Tell me, if that thou rightly ken,

When must Will Stutely die,

Who is one of bold Robins men,

一齐出发离开绿林，

决心要把维尔救回，

否则大家甘愿捐命。

9

他们来到城堡附近，

维尔就关押在那里面。

"我有个好主意，"罗宾汉说，

"咱们可在此埋下伏兵。

10

"然后派人去见行脚僧，

向他探听一下虚实。

那人就站在城堡下，

也许能提供点信息。"

11

一位勇敢的年轻人，

马上向着城堡走去。

他这样对行脚僧说：

"老大爷，有事恳求你，

12

"如果你知道，请告诉我，

斯塔特利将在何时处死？

他是罗宾手下的人，

And here doth prisoner lie?

13

"Alack, alass," the palmer said,
    "And for ever wo is me!
Will Stutely hanged must be this day,
    On yonder gallows-tree.

14

"O had his noble master known,
    Hee would some succour send;
A few of his bold yeomandree
    Full soon would fetch him hence."

15

"I, that is true," the young man said;
    "I, that is true," said hee;
"Or, if they were neer to this place,
    They soon would set him free.

16

"But fare thou well, thou good old man,
    Farewell, and thanks to thee;
If Stutely hanged be this day,
    Revengd his death will be."

如今关押在牢房里。"

13

"哎呀,哎呀,"行脚僧说,

　　"这事我深感不幸!

斯塔特利今天就要处死,

　　绞刑架已设在那边。

14

"他的头领如果知道,

　　一定会前来营救。

英雄好汉只要来几位,

　　准能将死囚劫走。"

15

"嗨,这话不错,"年轻人说,

　　"你这话讲得很对头,

如果他们就在附近,

　　定能使他重获自由。

16

"再见,好心的老大爷,

　　再见,我十分感谢你;

如果斯塔特利今天被绞死,

　　自有人为他报仇雪恨。"

17

He was no sooner from the palmer gone,

    But the gates was opened wide,

And out of the castle Will Stutely came,

    Guarded on every side.

18

When hee was forth from the castle come,

    And saw no help was nigh,

Thus he did say unto the sheriff,

    Thus he said gallantly:

19

Now seeing that I needs must die,

    Orant me one boon, says he;

For my noble master nere had man

    That yet was hangd on the tree.

20

Give me a sword all in my hand,

    And let mee be unbound,

And with thee and thy men I'le fight,

    Vntill I lie dead on the ground.

21

But his desire he would not grant,

17

他刚从行脚僧处返回，
　　城堡的大门已经洞开。
维尔从里面被押解而出，
　　左右两边都有人防卫。

18

维尔被押着走出城堡，
　　发现没有人来救他，
便勇敢地面对那郡长，
　　道出了下列一番话：

19

"既然今天横竖是一死，
　　请让我选择一种死法。
我的头领品德高尚，
　　他的人从没上过绞架。

20

"请求你给我一把剑，
　　然后再给我松绑。
让我跟你们大家厮杀，
　　直到战死在这片土地上。"

21

这要求没有得到允许，

His wishes were in vain;

For the sheriff had sworn he hanged should be,

And not by the sword be slain.

22

"Do but unbind my hands," he saies,

　"I will no weapons crave,

And if I hanged be this day,

　Damnation let me have."

23

"O no, O no," the sheriff he said,

　"Thou shalt on the gallows die,

I, and so shall thy master too,

　If ever in me it lie."

24

"O dastard coward!" Stutely cries,

　"Thou faint-heart pesant slave!

If ever my master do thee meet,

　Thou shalt thy paiment have.

25

"My noble master thee doth scorn,

　And all thy cowardly crew;

Such silly imps unable are

维尔的愿望成了泡影；
郡长坚持要把他绞死，
　　而不用剑取他生命。

22

"那就松松绑吧，"维尔又说，
　　"我不再要求任何武器，
如果要我绞架上受死，
　　那是存心罚我下地狱。"

23

"不行不行，"郡长说，
　　"你一定得受绞刑，
你的头领一旦落网，
　　也一样绞架上送命。"

24

"胆小鬼!"维尔大声骂道，
　　"你的心胸脆弱而狭隘!
如果碰上我的头领，
　　一定向你讨还血债。

25

"你这样的孬种懦夫，
　　我的头领最为蔑视；
如此愚蠢的小魔鬼，

Bold Robin to subdue."

26

But when he was to the gallows come,
　And ready to bid adiew,
Out of a bush leaps Little John,
　And steps Will Stutely to.

27

"I pray thee, Will, before thou die,
　Of thy dear friends take leave;
I needs must borrow him a while,
　How say you, master sheriff?"

28

"Now, as I live," the sheriff he said,
　"That varlet will I know;
Some sturdy rebell is that same,
　Therefore let him not go."

29

With that Little John so hastily
　A way cut Stutely's bands,
And from one of the sheriff his men,
　A sword twicht from his hands.

万难将罗宾汉征服!"

26

维尔走到绞架跟前,

　　正要同观众说再见,

树丛中蹿出小约翰,

　　疾步来到他身边。

27

"维尔,我有一事求你,

　　临死前跟你的好友辞个行;

郡长老爷,这人我借一会儿,

　　不知你有没有意见?"

28

"只要我活着,"郡长说,

　　"就要追查这个恶寇;

许多暴乱就这样开始,

　　留心别让这家伙逃走!"

29

小约翰动作极其敏捷,

　　维尔的绑绳已被他割掉;

接着他从郡长随从那里,

　　劈手夺过一柄宝剑。

30

"Here, Will, here, take thou this same,
  Thou canst it better sway;
And here defend thy self a while,
  For aid will come straight way."

31

And there they turnd them back to back,
  In the middle of them that day,
Till Robin Hood approached neer,
  With many an archer gay.

32

With that an arrow by them flew,
  I wist from Robin Hood;
"Make haste, make haste," the sheriff he said,
  "Make haste, for it is good."

33

The sheriff is gone; his doughty men
  Thought it no boot to stay,
But, as their master had them taught,
  They run full fast away.

30

"维尔,拿住这把剑,

　　虽然你还不能挥舞得更好,

但现在需要用它防身,

　　接应的人马很快赶到。"

31

两人背靠背协同作战,

　　郡长的人把他们围在中央,

直到许多快活的弓箭手,

　　在罗宾统率下投入战场。

32

他们首先射来一支箭,

　　射箭的正是罗宾自己。

"快撤!快撤!"郡长叫道,

　　"快撤,现在还来得及。"

33

郡长一拍屁股逃走,

　　他的勇士也就无心恋战。

他们遵照郡长的指令,

　　夹起尾巴四下逃窜。

34

"O stay, O stay," Will Stutely said,

"Take leave ere you depart;

You nere will catch bold Robin Hood

Vnless you dare him meet."

35

"O ill betide you," quoth Robin Hood,

"That you so soon are gone;

My sword may in the scabbord rest,

For here our work is done."

36

"I little thought when I came here,

When I came to this place,

For to have met with Little John,

Or seen my masters face."

37

Thus Stutely was at liberty set,

And safe brought from his foe;

"O thanks, O thanks to my master,

Since here it was not so."

34

"站住!站住!"维尔喊道,

　　"分手前应打个招呼;

你们不敢见见罗宾汉,

　　就永远别想把他逮住。"

35

"该死的家伙,"罗宾汉说,

　　"你们逃起命来倒迅速;

我的剑只好插回鞘里,

　　因为战斗已告结束。"

36

维尔说:"当我被押到这里,

　　总以为死神已在眼前,

没想到能见到小约翰,

　　更没想到能见到头领。"

37

就这样,维尔重获自由,

　　从仇敌手里安全脱险。

"千恩万谢我的头领,

　　没有他不会有我今天。"

38

"And once again, my fellows,

    We shall in the green woods meet,

Where we will make our bow-strings twang,

    Musick for us most sweet."

38

"伙计们,"罗宾汉说,

　"咱们将重聚在绿林,

在那里将弓弦绷紧,

　弹奏出最优美的乐音。"

ROBIN HOOD RESCUING
THREE SQUIRES

1

THERE are twelve months in all the year,
   As I hear many men say,
But the merriest month in all the year
   Is the merry month of May.

2

Now Robin Hood is to Nottingham gone,
   With a link a down and a day,
And there he met a silly old woman,
   Was weeping on the way.

3

"What news? what news, thou silly old woman?
   What news hast thou for me?"
Said she, There's three squires in Nottingham town
   To-day is condemned to die.

4

"O have they parishes burnt?" he said,
   "Or have they ministors slain?

罗宾汉劫法场

1

一年共有十二个月，
　我听人们都这么说。
一年中最美好的季节，
　当推乐融融的五月。

2

罗宾汉前往诺丁汉，
　喂斯呃令呃喤呃喤，
路遇一位可怜的老妇，
　呜呜啼哭在道路旁。

3

"你为何伤心，老婆婆？
　能不能跟我谈谈？"
"我有三个儿子，"她说，
　"今天要被处死在诺丁汉。"

4

"他们有没有纵火烧村庄？
　有没有谋杀过教长？

Or have they robbed any virgin,

Or with other men's wives have lain?"

5

"They have no parishes burnt, good sir,

Nor yet have ministers slain,

Nor have they robbed any virgin,

Nor with other men's wives have lain."

6

"O what have they done?" said bold Robin Hood,

"I pray thee tell to me:"

"It's for slaying of the king's fallow deer,

Bearing their long bows with thee."

7

"Dost thou not mind, old woman," he said,

"Since thou made me sup and dine?

By the truth of my body," quoth bold Robin Hood,

You could not tell it in better time."

8

Now Robin Hood is to Nottingham gone,

With a link a down and a day,

And there he met with a silly old palmer,

Was walking along the highway.

有没有抢劫过少女？

　　有没有霸占过他人妻房？"

5

"先生，他们没有纵火烧村庄，

　　没有谋杀过教长，

没有抢劫过少女，

　　没有霸占过他人妻房。"

6

"哟，他们到底犯什么罪？"

　　勇敢的罗宾汉问，"请你告诉我。"

"他们随身带着弓箭，

　　猎杀过国王的红鹿。"

7

"你记得吧，"罗宾汉说，

　　"先前我受过你的款待？

今凭这血肉之躯做证，

　　你诉说冤情适逢其会。"

8

罗宾汉前往诺丁汉，

　　喂斯呃令呃噎呃噎，

路遇一位可怜的行脚僧，

　　沿着大道踉跄前行。

9

"What news? what news, thou silly old man?
 What news, I do thee pray?"
Said he, Three squires in Nottingham town
 Are condemnd to die this day.

10

"Come change thy apparel with me, old man,
 Come change thy apparel for mine;
Here is forty shillings in good silver,
 Go drink it in beer or wine."

11

"O thine apparel is good," he said,
 "And mine is ragged and torn;
Wherever you go, wherever you ride,
 Laugh neer an old man to scorn."

12

"Come change thy apparel with me, old churl,
 Come change thy apparel with mine;
Here are twenty pieces of good broad gold,
 Go feast thy brethren with wine."

13

Then he put on the old man's hat,

9

"出了什么事,老爷爷?
　能不能跟我谈谈?"
"今天有三位绅士,"他说,
　"要被处死在诺丁汉。"

10

"老爷爷,过来换换衣裳,
　过来跟我换换衣裳;
这里有四十先令银币,
　拿去弄点好酒尝尝。"

11

"哟,你的衣裳那么好,
　我的衣裳却这么糟;
不管你骑马到那里,
　千万别拿老人取笑。"

12

"快过来换衣裳吧,老糊涂,
　快过来跟我换衣裳,
这里再给你二十枚大金币,
　供你宴请自家的兄长。"

13

他戴上老人的帽子,

It stood full high on the crown:
"The first bold bargain that I come at,
It shall make thee come down."

14

Then he put on the old man's cloak,
Was patchd black, blew, and red;
He thought no shame all the day long
To wear the bags of bread.

15

Then he put on the old man's breeks,
Was patchd from ballup to side;
"By the truth of my body," bold Robin can say,
"This man lovd little pride."

16

Then he put on the old man's hose,
Were patchd from knee to wrist;
"By the truth of my body," said bold Robin Hood,
"I'd laugh if I had any list."

17

Then he put on the old man's shoes,
Were patchd both beneath and aboon;
Then Robin Hood swore a solemn oath,

那帽子高耸在头顶：
"我做成这头桩生意
　要是你准得陪光老本。"

14

他披上老人的外氅，
　那外氅补缀得五色斑斓；
他觉得虽然整天背着面包袋，
　也用不着自愧自惭。

15

他穿上老人的马裤，
　那马裤处处经过缝补。
"凭这血肉之躯做证，"罗宾汉说，
　"这人日子过得真寒苦。"

16

他穿上老人的长筒袜，
　那袜子上下都经过缝补，
"凭这血肉之躯做证，"罗宾汉说，
　"谁真喜欢它那才要笑掉牙。"

17

他穿上老人的鞋子，
　那鞋子前后补丁缀满，
罗宾汉庄严地发誓说：

It's good habit that makes a man.

18

Now Robin Hood is to Nottingham gone,

With a link a down and a down,

And there he met with the prond sheriff,

Was walking along the town.

19

"O save, O save, O sheriff," he said,

"O save, and you may see!

And what will you give to a silly old man

To-day will your hangman be?"

20

"Some suits, some suits," the sheriff he said,

"Some suits I'll give to thee;

Some suits, some suits, and pence thirteen

To-day's a hangman's fee."

21

Then Robin he turns him round about,

And jumps from stock to stone;

"By the truth of my body," the sheriff he said,

"That's well jumpt, thou nimble old man."

"人还真要靠衣服装扮。"

18

罗宾汉前往诺丁汉，

　　喂斯呃令呃噌呃噌，

在那里遇见傲慢的郡长，

　　正行走在去刑场的路上。

19

"行行好吧，郡长，"罗宾汉说，

　　"我这可怜相你已看到；

请问你给我施舍点什么？

　　今天行刑手犒赏有多少？"

20

"几套衣裳，几套衣裳，"郡长说，

　　"我将施舍你几套衣裳，

另外再加十三便士，

　　便是今天行刑手的犒赏。"

21

罗宾汉朝周围看了看，

　　从行刑架跳到台阶上。

"凭我血肉之躯做证，"郡长说，

　　"你这老头身手倒不凡。"

22

"I was neer a haugman in all my life,
  Nor yet intends to trade;
But curst be he," said bold Robin,
  "That first a hangman was made.

23

"I've a bag for meal, and a bag for malt,
  And a bag for barley and corn;
A bag for bread, and a bag for beef,
  And a bag for my little small horn.

24

"I have a horn in my pocket,
  I got it from Robin Hood,
And still when I set it to my mouth,
  For thee it blows little good."

25

"O wind thy horn, thou proud fellow,
  Of thee I have no doubt;
I wish that thou give such a blast
  Till both thy eyes fall out."

26

The first loud blast that he did blow,

22

"我一生从没有做过行刑手[6]，
　　今天更无意将这恶差揽兜，
谁最初做这公干，"罗宾汉说，
　　"谁就该受到诅咒。

23

"我随身带着许多口袋，
　　用来盛吃喝，盛谷物；
此外还有面包袋、牛肉袋、
　　安放小号角的号角袋。

24

"号角就藏在这只口袋里，
　　这玩意我得之于罗宾汉。
如果为你将它放到嘴边吹，
　　那声音一定嘹亮悠扬。"

25

"那就吹吧，傲慢的家伙，
　　不信你能耍什么花招，
我希望你憋足劲儿吹，
　　直吹得眼珠子爆掉。"

26

罗宾汉吹响第一声号角，

He blew both loud and shrill;

A hundred and fifty of Robin Hood's men

Came riding over the hill.

27

The next loud blast that he did give,

He blew both loud and amain,

And quickly sixty of Robin Hood's men

Came shining over the plain.

28

"O who are you," the sheriff he said,

"Come tripping over the lee?"

"The're my attendants," brave Robin did say,

"Ther'll pay a visit to thee."

29

They took the gallows from the slack,

They set it in the glen,

They hangd the proud sheriff on that,

Releasd their own three men.

那声音尖锐而嘹亮；
他手下一百五十名好汉，
　骑着马奔下了山冈。

27
罗宾汉吹响第二声号角，
　那声音清脆而舒畅；
他手下六十名壮士，
　雄赳赳出现在田野上。

28
"哟，那骑马奔驰在对面草地的，"
　郡长问，"是什么人？"
"他们是我的随从，"罗宾汉说，
　"专程前来拜访你。"

29
他们从峡谷中抬出绞刑架，
　把它安置在一块空地上。
傲慢的郡长被吊了上去，
　三个死囚获得释放。

ROBIN HOOD AND
GUY OF GISBORNE

1

WHEN shawes beenesheene, and shradds full fayre,

And leeues both large and longe,

Itt is merry, walking in the fayre forrest,

To heare the small birds songe.

2

The woodweele sang, and wold not cease,

Amongst the leaues a lyne:

And it is by two wight yeomen,

By deare God, that I meane.

3

"Me thought they did mee beate and binde,

And tooke my bow mee froe;

If I bee Robin a-liue in this lande,

I'le be wrocken on both them towe."

4

"Sweauens are swift, master," quoth John,

"As the wind that blowes ore a hill;

罗宾汉与
吉斯本的盖尔

1

丛林里美丽灿烂，

　　树叶子郁郁苍苍；

人在绿林中漫游，

　　听鸟鸣心情舒畅。

2

在椴树的浓荫下，

　　云雀不停地歌唱。

哎哟，老天爷做证，

　　那边来了两位大汉。

3

"我记得他们打我绑我，

　　还把我的弓箭夺走；

只要我罗宾汉活在世上，

　　就一定向他们报仇。"

4

"头领，梦转瞬即逝，"约翰说，

　　"一如那狂风吹过山冈；

For if itt be neuer soe lowde this night,

    To-morrow it may be still."

5

"Buske yee, bowne yee, my merry men all,

    For John shall goe with mee;

For I'le goe seeke yond wight yeomen

    In green-wood where the bee."

6

The cast on their gowne of greene,

    A shooting gone are they,

Vntill they came to the merry green-wood,

    Where they had gladdest bee;

There were the ware of [a] wight yeoman,

    His body leaned to a tree.

7

A sword and a dagger he wore by his side,

    Had beene many a mans bane,

And he was cladd in his capull-hyde,

    Topp, and tayle, and mayne.

8

"Stand you still, master," quoth Little John,

    "Vnder this trusty tree,

别看它今晚呼啸正急，

　　到明天又会宁静安然。"

5

"伙计们，大家分头行动，

　　我与约翰要出去一趟，

在他们所在的绿林里，

　　寻找梦中的两位壮汉。"

6

他俩披上绿色披风，

　　行走得急急匆匆，

一直来到美丽的绿林，

　　惊喜之情油然而生：

只见那里确有个壮汉，

　　身子就靠在大树边。

7

这人身佩匕首与宝剑，

　　许多人曾死在他手里。

只见他身披马革盔甲，

　　模样既魁梧又壮实。

8

"头领，请你止步，"小约翰说，

　　"请你在这树下休息，

And I will goe to yond wight yeoman,

To know his meaning trulye."

9

"A, John, by me thou setts noe store,

And that's a farley thinge;

How offt send I my men beffore,

And tarry my-selfe behinde?

10

"It is noe cunning a knaue to ken,

And a man but heare him speake;

And itt were not for bursting of my bowe,

John, I wold thy head breake."

11

But often words they breeden bale,

That parted Robin and John;

John is gone to Barn[e]sdale,

The gates he knowes eche one.

12

And when hee came to Baruesdale,

Great heauinesse there hee hadd;

He found two of his fellowes

Were slaine both in a slade,

我先去会会那壮汉，

　　试探一下他的来意。”

9

“约翰，我真要看轻你，

　　你的话太没个道理。

何时我只派侍从出阵，

　　自己却在后面躲避？

10

“体察下情其实容易，

　　闻其言便知其心理。

要不是怕把弓折断，

　　我会砸破你的头皮。”

11

言辞不当招灾惹祸，

　　罗宾与约翰分道扬镳。

约翰前往巴恩斯代尔，

　　那里的路径他了如指掌。

12

当他来到巴恩斯代尔，

　　心里顿觉万分悲伤。

他发现两个绿林伙伴，

　　被杀害在一片沼地之上。

13

And Scarlet a foote flyinge was,

Ouer stockes and stone,

For the sheriffe with seuen score men

Fast after him is gone.

14

"Yett one shoote I'le shoote," sayes Little John,

"With Crist his might and mayne;

I'le make yond fellow that flyes soe fast

To be both glad and faine."

15

John bent vp a good veiwe bow,

And fetteled him to shoote;

The bow was made of a tender boughe,

And fell downe to his foote.

16

"Woe worth thee, wicked wood," sayd Little John,

"That ere thou grew on a tree!

For this day thou art my bale,

My boote when thou shold bee!"

17

This shoote it was but looselye shott,

13

斯盖莱特缺肢残体地躺着，

　　背垫着石块与紫罗兰，

刚才郡长亲率百余人，

　　在他背后紧紧追赶。

14

"以牙还牙，"小约翰说，

　　"我主基督威力无边，

我要让匆匆离开的伙伴，

　　有泉之下含笑长眠。"

15

小约翰拉开紫杉弓，

　　打算将箭射向郡长；

但紫衫树枝不够坚韧，

　　折断后掉落在脚旁。

16

"该死的木头，"小约翰骂道，

　　"你不该生长在树上！

今天坏了我的正事，

　　使我不能如愿以偿。"

17

这箭摇摇摆摆飞出去，

The arrowe flew in vaine,

And it mett one of the sheriffes men;

Good William a Trent was slaine.

18

It had beene better for William a Trent

To hange vpon a gallowe

Then for to lye in the green-wood,

There slaine with an arrowe.

19

And it is sayd, when men be mett,

Six can doe more then three:

And they haue tane Little John,

And bound him flast to a tree.

20

"Thou shalt be drawen by dale and dowue," quoth the sheriffe,

"And hanged hye on a hill:"

"But thou may fayle," quoth Little John,

"If itt be Christs owne will."

21

Let vs leaue talking of Little John,

For hee is bound fast to a tree,

And talke of Guy and Robin Hood,

没有射在郡长身上，
却射中他手下一人，
　好心的威廉·却特一命呜呼。

18

对于威廉·却特来说，
　与其如此被箭射中丧命，
暴尸在葱绿的林间，
　还不如上绞架死于绞刑。

19

我们知道，在战场上，
　人多毕竟力量更大，
他们终于把小约翰抓住，
　牢牢地绑到一棵树上。

20

"让穷鬼拉走你!"郡长说，
　"在山坡上高高吊起!"
"你会失算的，"小约翰说，
　"除非那是上帝旨意。"

21

小约翰被捆绑在树上，
　这事暂且搁下不提。
回头再说盖尔与罗宾汉，

In the green-wood where they bee.

22

How these two yeomen together they mett,

Vnder the leaues of lyne,

To see what marchandise they made

Euen at that same time.

23

"Good morrow, good fellow," quoth Sir Guy;

"Good morrow, good fellow," quoth hee;

"Methinkes by this bow thou beares in thy hand,

A good archer thou seems to bee."

24

"I am wilfull of my way," quoth Sir Guye,

"And of my morning tyde:"

"I'le lead thee through the wood," quoth Robin,

"Good fellow, I'le be thy guide."

25

"I seeke an outlaw," quoth Sir Guye,

"Men call him Robin Hood;

I had rather meet with him vpon a day

Then forty pound of golde."

两人都还在绿林里。

22

在椴树的浓荫下，
    不知他俩如何格斗，
在刚才这段时间里，
    究竟那鹿死在谁手？

23

"早安,好伙计!"盖尔爵士说。
    "早安,好伙计!"罗宾汉回答,
"你手上拿着一把弓,
    看样儿是好射手。"

24

"我迷了路,"盖尔爵士说,
    "还弄不清现在是上午还是下午。"
"我带你走出树林,"罗宾汉说,
    "好伙计,让我给你指路。"

25

"我在追捕一个法外人,"盖尔说,
    "人们管他叫罗宾汉,
我真恨不得有天碰上他,
    那时就有赏金四十镑。"

26

"If you tow mett, itt wold be seene whether were better
    Afore yee did part awaye;
Let vs some other pastime find,
    Good fellow, I thee pray.

27

"Let vs some other masteryes make,
    And wee will walke in the woods euen;
Wee may chance mee[t] with Robin Hood
    Att some vnsett steven."

28

They cutt them downe the summer shroggs
    Which grew both vnder a bryar,
And sett them three score rood in twinn,
    To shoote the prickes full neare.

29

"Leade on, good fellow," sayd Sir Guye,
    "Lead on, I doe bidd thee:"
"Nay, by my faith," quoth Robin Hood,
    "The leader thou shalt bee."

30

The first good shoot that Robin ledd

26

"如果你俩碰在一起，
  分手前准得比个高低。
好伙计，我请求你，
  咱们也要要什么游戏。

27

"让咱们先比比武艺，
  然后再进入宁静的林地。
说不定在某个时候，
  就会跟罗宾汉碰在一起。"

28

他们在一株石楠下，
  砍掉两丛落叶灌木，
然后站开六十杆远，
  看谁能射中那株树。

29

"射吧，好伙计，"盖尔爵士说，
  "射吧，我在等着你。"
"不，我发誓，"罗宾汉说，
  "这箭应让你先射。"

30

最后还是罗宾先射，

Did not shoote an inch the pricke froe;

Guy was an archer good enoughe,

But he cold neere shoote soe.

31

The second shoote Sir Guy shott,

He shott within the garlande;

But Robin Hood shott it better than hee,

For he cloue the good pricke-wande.

32

"Gods blessing on thy heart!" sayes Guye,

"Goode fellow, thy shooting is goode;

For an thy hart be as good as thy hands,

Thou were better then Robin Hood."

33

"Tell me thy name, good fellow," quoth Guy,

"Vnder the leanes of lyne;"

"Nay, by my faith," quoth good Robin,

"Till thou haue told me thine."

34

"I dwell by dale and downe," quoth Guye,

"And I haue done many a curst trune;

And he that calles me by my right name

他的箭不偏不倚正中树干。
盖尔虽然是个好射手，
　　百发百中却谈不上。

31

盖尔接着射第三箭，
　　那箭也落在圈子内。
但罗宾汉的箭射得更好，
　　因为那箭正中靶心。

32

"主赐福你，"盖尔爵士说，
　　"好伙计，你身手不凡，
想射哪里就射哪里，
　　连那罗宾汉也比不上。"

33

"在这椴树的浓荫下，"盖尔说，
　　"好伙计，请通报你的姓名。"
"不行，老天做证，"罗宾汉说，
　　"我得先知道你的姓名。"

34

"我日子过得潦倒，"盖尔说，
　　"受人诅咒的事干过不少。
若要问我的真姓实名，

Calles me Guye of good Gysborne."

35

"My dwelling is in the wood," sayes Robin;

  "By thee I set right nought;

My name is Robin Hood of Barnesdale,

  A fellow thou has long sought."

36

He that had neither beene a kithe nor kin

  Might haue seene a full fayre sight,

To see how together these yeomen went,

  With blades both browne and bright.

37

To haue seene how these yeomen together foug[ht],

  Two howers of a summers day;

Itt was neither Guy nor Robin Hood

  That fettled them to flye away.

38

Robin was rencheles on a roote,

  And stumbled at that tyde,

And Guy was quicke and nimble withall,

  And hitt him ore the left side.

可叫我吉斯本的盖尔。"

35

"我居住在林地,"罗宾汉说,

　　"谅你不能把我怎么样;

我就是你想拿获的人,

　　人称巴恩斯代尔的罗宾汉。"

36

我的同胞与父老乡亲,

　　恐怕从没见过这场面,

两位斗士走到一块,

　　手中提着闪亮的宝剑。

37

他俩在一起拼死格斗,

　　夏日里但闻声声高吼;

不论是盖尔还是罗宾,

　　谁也不想轻易逃走。

38

罗宾汉没留神一条树根,

　　双脚一绊没能站稳。

盖尔动作十分敏捷,

　　一剑刺中他的左身。

39

"Ah, deere Lady!" sayd Robin Hood,
   "Thou art both mother and may!
I thinke it was neuer mans destinye
   To dye before his day."

40

Robin thought on Our Lady deere,
   And soone leapt vp againe,
And thus he came with an awkwarde stroke;
   Good Sir Guy hee has slayne.

41

He tooke Sir Guys head by the hayre,
   And sticked itt on his bowes end:
"Thou hast beene traytor all thy liffe,
   Which thing must haue an ende."

42

Robin pulled forth an Irish kniffe,
   And nicked Sir Guy in the face,
That hee was neuer on a woman borne
   Cold tell who Sir Guye was.

43

Saies, Lye there, lye there, good Sir Guye,

39

"圣母呀,"罗宾汉叫道,

　　"你既是处女又是母亲,

我想一个人大限未到,

　　总不该如此丢掉性命。"

40

罗宾汉一想到圣母,

　　即刻从地上一跃而起,

随即给对方狠狠一剑,

　　盖尔的人头便已落地。

41

他拾起盖尔的头,

　　把它缚在长弓上。

"你一生作恶多端,

　　让你有个该有的下场。"

42

罗宾汉拔出一把爱尔兰刀,

　　在盖尔脸上划了几道痕,

凡是母胎所生之人,

　　再也难把盖尔辨认。

43

"躺着吧,英勇的盖尔爵士,

And with me be not wrothe;

If thou haue had the worse stroakes at my hand,

Thou shalt haue the better cloathe.

44

Robin did off his gowne of greene,

Sir Guye hee did it throwe;

And hee put on that capull-hyde,

That cladd him topp to toe.

45

"The bowe, the arrowes, and litle horne,

And with me now I'le beare;

For now I will goe to Barn[e]sdale,

To see how my men doe fare."

46

Robin sett Guyes horne to his mouth,

A lowd blast in it he did blow;

That beheard the sheriffe of Nottingham,

As he leaned vnder a lowe.

47

"Hearken! hearken!" sayd the sheriffe,

"I heard noe tydings but good;

For yonder I heare Sir Guyes horne blowe,

用不着向我报仇雪耻，
刚才如能砍伤我的手，
　　就不会弄成这副样子。"

44

罗宾脱下身上的绿衣，
　　将它留给盖尔爵士。
并换下他的马革盔甲，
　　从上到下打扮自己。

45

"他的弓箭,还有这号角，
　　我要全部带在身上。
现在该去巴恩斯代尔，
　　看看约翰干得怎么样。"

46

罗宾将盖尔的号角放到嘴边，
　　吹出一阵嘹亮声音。
诺丁汉郡长就站在山脚下，
　　及时听到那阵号角声。

47

"快听,快听!"郡长说，
　　"我听见那边传来佳音，
盖尔爵士吹响号角，

For he hath slaine Robin Hood.

48

"For yonder I heare Sir Guyes horne blow,
    Itt blowes soe well in tyde,
For yonder comes that wighty yeoman,
    Cladd in his capull-hyde.

49

"Come hither, thou good Sir Guy,
    Aske of mee what thou wilt haue:"
"I'le none of thy gold," sayes Robin Hood,
    "Nor I'le none of itt haue."

50

"But now I haue slaine the master," he sayd,
    "Let me goe strike the knaue;
This is all the reward I aske,
    Nor noe other will I haue."

51

"Thou art a madman," said the shiriffe,
    "Thou sholdest haue had a knights fee;
Seeing thy asking [hath] beene soe badd,
    Well granted it shall be."

他一定干掉了罗宾。

48

"盖尔爵士吹响号角，
　　吹得及时,吹得嘹亮!
瞧,我的勇士下山了,
　　马革盔甲披在身上。

49

"上这儿来,我的好盖尔,
　　你要我给点什么奖励?"
"我不要你的金子,"罗宾说,
　　"我不想得到任何东西。"

50

"匪首已经杀死,"罗宾汉说,
　　"让我再去收拾那些苍头,
这就是我想得到的报酬,
　　别的一概无意恳求。"

51

"你是不是疯了?"郡长说,
　　"你应得到骑士的奖励,
这要求实在太糟糕,
　　但要答应倒也容易。"

52

But Little John heard his master speake,

　　Well he knew that was his steuen;

"Now shall I be loset," quoth Little John,

　　"With Christs might in heauen."

53

But Robin hee hyed him towards Little John,

　　Hee thought hee wold loose him beliue;

The sheriffe and all his companye

　　Fast after him did driue.

54

"Stand abacke! stand abacke!" sayd Robin;

　　"Why draw you mee soe neere?

Itt was neuer the vse in our countrye

　　One's shrift another shold heere."

55

But Robin pulled forth an Irysh kniffe,

　　And losed John hand and foote,

And gaue him Sir Guyes bow in his hand,

　　And bade it be his boote.

56

But John tooke Guyes bow in his hand—

52

小约翰听见头领在说话，

　那声音他熟悉非常。

"基督在天做证，"他说，

　"我将很快获得释放。"

53

罗宾快步走向小约翰，

　恨不得马上把他释放。

郡长率领他的人马，

　在他背后紧紧追赶。

54

"站住，站住!"罗宾汉说，

　"你们为什么向我靠近?

要随心所欲摆布别人，

　在我们这儿绝对不行。"

55

罗宾汉拔出爱尔兰宝刀，

　割断约翰手脚上的绑绳。

然后递过盖尔的大弓，

　让约翰用它来拒敌防身。

56

约翰将弓提在手里，

His arrowes were rawstye by the roote—;

The sherriffe saw Little John draw a bow

And fettle him to shoote.

57

Towards his house in Nottingham

He fled full fast away,

And soe did all his companye,

Not one behind did stay.

58

But he cold neither soe fast goe,

Nor away soe fast runn,

But Little John, with an arrow broade,

Did cleaue his heart in twinn.

那箭镞个个沾满血迹，
郡长看见约翰拉开弓，
　　正准备向他射出箭来。

57
郡长赶紧掉头而走，
　　想逃回诺丁汉他的家。
他手下那班子人马，
　　没有一个愿意留下。

58
郡长逃命本事不大，
　　郡长奔跑速度太慢，
小约翰射来的箭，
　　早穿透他的胸膛。

THE KING'S DISGUISE, AND FRIENDSHIP WITH ROBIN HOOD

1

KING RICHARD hearing of the pranks
  Of Robin Hood and his men,
He much admir'd, and more desir'd,
  To see both him and them.

2

Then with a dozen of his lords
  To Nottingham he rode;
When he came there, he made good cheer,
  And took up his abode.

3

He having staid there some time,
  But had no hopes to speed,
He and his lords, with [free] accord,
  All put on monk's weeds.

4

From Fountain-abby they did ride,

罗宾汉受招安

1

罗宾汉与众英雄的事迹，

　　传到国王理查耳边[7]。

他对他们无比钦佩，

　　一心想去亲眼见见。

2

他亲率十来位勋爵，

　　骑马向诺丁汉进发；

到达后便设宴洗尘，

　　安顿行宫歇鞍住下。

3

国王不想仓促行事，

　　一住住了好些日子。

然后与他的王公大臣，

　　各自换上僧侣服饰。

4

他们在芳汀寺上马起程，

Down to Barnsdale;

Where Robin Hood preparëd stood

All company to assail.

5

The king was higher then the rest,

And Robin thought he had

An abbot been whom he did spleen;

To rob him he was glad.

6

He took the king's horse by the head,

"Abbot," says he, "abide;

I am bound to rue such knaves as you,

That live in pomp and pride."

7

"But we are messengers from the king,"

The king himself did say;

"Near to this place his royal Grace

To speak with thee does stay."

8

"God save the king," said Robin Hood,

"And all that wish him well;

He that does deny his sovereignty,

进入巴恩斯代尔丛林。
罗宾汉早在路上等候，
　准备拦劫这班人。

5

国王身材比别人高大，
　罗宾当他就是院长。
这种人他恨之入骨，
　这次存心抢他一抢。

6

他挡住国王的马头，
　"哎，院长，请停一停，
你们这班家伙神气活现，
　我一定得收点买路钱。"

7

"我们是国王的使者，"
　国王自己这么声称，
"此次奉旨来到贵处，
　传谕他的赦免令。"

8

"愿主保佑国王，"罗宾汉说，
　"愿主保佑拥戴他的人；
谁要否认他的王权，

I wish he was in hell."

9

"O thyself thou curses," says the king,

"For thou a traitor art:"

"Nay, but that you are his messenger,

I swear you he lie heart.

10

"For I never yet hurt any man

That honest is and true;

But those that give their minds to live

Upon other men's due.

11

"I never hurt the husbandman,

That use to till the ground;

Nor spill their blood that range the wood

To follow hawk or hound.

12

"My chiefest spite to elergy is,

Who in these days bear a great sway;

With fryars and monks, with their fine sprunks,

I make my chiefest prey.

我就诅咒他下地狱。”

9

“你该诅咒自己,”国王说,

　“因为你才是叛臣贼党。”

“如果你是他的使者,”罗宾汉说,

　“我敢说你一定在撒谎。

10

“凡是诚实而善良的人,

　我决不会轻易伤害;

但如果他敲诈别人,

　我就决心跟他作对。

11

“农夫在田里耕作劳苦,

　绝不会受我随意荼毒;

猎人带鹰犬出没山林,

　也不会遭我无端杀戮。

12

“我最痛恨那班牧师,

　当今他们威风凛凛,

什么修士、僧侣、高贵的信徒,

　我要抢劫的正是这班人。

13

"But I am very glad," says Robin Hood,

 "That I have met you here;

Come, before we end, you shall, my friend,

 Taste of our green-wood cheer."

14

The king did then marvel much,

 And so did all his men;

They thought with fear, what kind of cheer

 Robin would provide for them.

15

Robin took the king's horse by the head,

 And led him to the tent;

"Thou would not be so usd," quoth he,

 "But that my king thee sent.

16

"Nay, more than that," said Robin Hood,

 "For good king Richard's sake,

If you had as much gold as ever I told,

 I would not one penny take."

17

Then Robin set his horn to his mouth,

13

"不过，今天见到诸位，
　我心里倒也其乐陶陶。
来吧，朋友，别忙着回去，
　请先去尝尝绿林的乳酪。"

14

国王心里惶恐不安，
　随从们个个提心吊胆。
他们担忧罗宾的乳酪，
　会不会有什么名堂。

15

罗宾拽住国王的马头，
　将他领进一顶营帐；
"我不会难为你，"罗宾汉说，
　"只因你派自我的国王。"

16

"你其实可以完全放心，
　为了仁慈的理查大帝，
只要你将钱如实申报，
　我决不拿你一个便士。"

17

罗宾汉把号角放到嘴边，

And a loud blast he did blow,

Till a hundred and ten of Robin Hood's men

Came marching all of a row.

18

And when they came hold Robin before,

Each man did bend his knee;

"O," thought the king, "'t is a gallant thing,

And a seemly sight to see."

19

Within himself the king did say,

These men of Robin Hood's

More humble be than mine to me;

So the court may learn of the woods.

20

So then they all to dinner went,

Upon a earpet green;

Black, yellow, red, finely minglëd,

Most curious to be seen.

21

Venison and fowls were plenty there,

With fish out of the river:

King Richard swore, on sea or shore,

吹出一阵嘹亮的声音，
他手下一百一十位壮士，
列队来到他跟前。

18

众壮士来到头领跟前，
一个个向他屈膝行礼。
"哟，真够气派，"国王想，
"这情景真不可思议。"

19

国王自言自语地说：
"罗宾汉手下这班人，
比我手下的还忠顺，
看来朝廷还得学绿林。"

20

在一片绿茸茸的草地上，
他们一道席地进餐。
刹那间五颜六色相映照，
看上去奇妙非常。

21

鹿肉、禽肉十分充足，
此外还有山涧鲜鱼。
国王说自己走南闯北，

He neer was feasted better.

22

Then Robin takes a can of ale:

   "Come, let us now begin;

Come, every man shall have his can;

   Here's a health unto the king."

23

The king himself drank to the king,

   So round about it went;

Two barrels of ale, both stout and stale,

   To pledge that health were spent.

24

And after that, a bowl of wine

   In his hand took Robin Hood;

"Unitl I die, I'll drink wine," said he,

   "While I live in the green-wood.

25

"Bend all your bows," said Robin Hood,

   "And with the grey goose wing

Such sport now shew as you would do

   In the presence of the king."

还从没吃得这样舒爽。

22

罗宾汉端起一罐麦酒:

　　"伙计们,让我们干杯吧,

请大家每人端起酒罐,

　　为了国王的健康干杯!"

23

国王为他自己干杯,

　　大伙轮番为国王祝颂;

用来干杯的玉液琼浆,

　　很快被人喝掉两大桶。

24

待到干杯的呼声平息,

　　罗宾汉又端起酒一碗,

"生活在绿林中,"他说,

　　"酒是我终生的伙伴。

25

"伙计们,把弓拉开,

　　插上灰色的鹅羽箭。

大家务必努力争胜,

　　仿佛就在国王面前。"

26

They shewd such brave archery,

    By cleaving sticks and wands,

That the king did say, Such men as they

    Live not in many lands.

27

"Well, Robin Hood," then says the king,

    "If I could thy pardon get,

To serve the king in every thing

    Wouldst thou thy mind firm set?"

28

"Yes, with all my heart," bold Robin said,

    So they flung off their hoods;

To serve the king in every thing,

    They swore they would spend their bloods.

29

"For a clergyman was first my bane,

    Which makes me hate them all;

But if you'll be so kind to me,

    Love them again I shall."

30

The king no longer could forbear,

26

他们射技高超非常，

　　箭无虚发百步穿杨。

国王见了开口说话：

　　"这样的射手天下罕见。"

27

"好啊，罗宾汉，"国王又说，

　　"假如我帮你获准赦免，

让你忠心为国王效劳，

　　不知你能否把主意拿定？"

28

"十分情愿，"勇敢的罗宾说。

　　他们将自己的帽子抛起，

发誓效忠他们的国王，

　　甘愿为他肝脑涂地。

29

"我受过一个牧师陷害，

　　这使我将他们恨透。

既然你待我如此友好，

　　我会跟他们释隙消仇。"

30

国王感动得顿生怜悯，

For he was movd with ruth;
"Robin," said he, "I now tell thee
The very naked truth."

31

"I am the king, thy sovereign king,
That appears before you all;"
When Robin see that it was he,
Strait then he down did fall.

32

"Stand up again," then said the king,
"I'll thee thy pardon give;
Stand up, my friend; who can contend,
When I give leave to live?"

33

So they are all gone to Nottingham,
All shouting as they came;
But when the people them did see,
They thought the king was slain,

34

And for that cause the outlaws were come,
To rule all as they list;
And for to shun, which way to run

这时再也忍耐不住：
"罗宾汉，我要把自己的身份，
　直截了当地告诉你。

31

"我就是国王，你们的君主，
　现在就站在大家跟前。"
罗宾汉一听他就是国王，
　赶紧跪倒泥首请罪。

32

"起来吧，朋友，"国王说，
　"你们的罪我一概赦免，
是我亲口答应你们，
　谁还敢再来争论？"

33

他们一道前往诺丁汉，
　一路上又欢呼又喝彩。
人们最初见到他们，
　还当国王已被杀害。

34

他们以为这班法外人，
　要来为所欲为逞凶狂；
于是人人惊惶失措，

The people did not wist.

35

The plowman left the plow in the fields,
    The smith ran from his shop;
Old folks also, that scarce could go,
    Over their sticks did hop.

36

The king soon let them understand
    He had been in the green-wood,
And from that day, for evermore,
    He'd forgiven Robin Hood.

37

When the people they did hear,
    And the truth was known,
They all did sing, "God save the king!
    Hang eare, the town's our own!"

38

"What's that Robin Hood?" then said the sheriff;
    "That varlet I do hate;
Both me and mine he causd to dine,
    And servd us all with one plate."

不知什么地方能躲藏。

35

农夫把犁耙丢在田里，
　　铁匠逃出打铁店。
即使行动不便的老人，
　　也拄着拐杖踉跄奔命。

36

国王马上告谕臣民，
　　说他刚从绿林回返，
从今后不论何时，
　　他都要宽宥罗宾汉。

37

人们听到这一消息，
　　这才明白事情真相。
他们欢呼："主庇护国王！
　　不必担忧，一切正常！"

38

"罗宾汉是什么人？"郡长问，
　　"我恨透了这个流氓。
他强迫我与随员进餐，
　　提供的饭菜却只有一盘。"

"Ho, ho," said Robin, "I know what you mean;
  Come, take your gold again;
Be friends with me, and I with thee,
  And so with every man.

"Now, master sheriff, you are paid,
  And since you are beginner,
As well as you give me my due;
  For you neer paid for that dinner.

"But if that it should please the king
  So much your house to grace
To sup with you, for to speak true,
  [I] know you neer was base."

The sheriff could not [that] gain say,
  For a trick was put upon him;
A supper was drest, the king was guest,
  But he thought't would have undone him.

They are all gone to London court,

39

"呵呵,我懂你的意思,"罗宾汉说,
　"来吧,我把金子归还你;
让咱们从此友好相处,
　让我们大家都成亲知。

40

"郡长老爷,钱已还清,
　和解就从你这里开始;
但属于我的也该归还,
　那顿晚宴你还没付账。

41

"如果这能使国王高兴,
　就请你在贵府设宴,
让我们同饮美酒,说真的,
　我知道你并非爱财如命。"

42

郡长明知自己受愚弄,
　但又不便争长论短。
宴席齐备,国王做客赴宴;
　郡长唯恐把钱花光。

43

罗宾汉与他的众壮士,

Robin Hood, with all his train;
He once was there a noble peer,
   And now he's there again.

44

Many such pranks brave Robin playd
   While he lived in the green wood:
Now, my friends, attend, and hear an end
   Of honest Robin Hood.

一道前往首都伦敦。
他曾经是那里的贵族，
　　而今又名正言顺。

44

罗宾汉生活在绿林，
　　胡闹戏谑的故事数不胜数。
朋友,关于诚实的罗宾,
　　今天的故事到此结束。

ROBIN HOOD'S
DEATH

1

WHEN Robin Hood and Little John
  Down a down a down a down
Went oer you bank of broom,
  Said Robin Hood bold to Little John,
We have shot for many a pound.
  Hey, etc.

2

But I am not able to shoot one shot more,
  My broad arrows will not flee;
But I have a cousin lives down below,
  Please God, she will bleed me.

3

Now Robin he is to fair Kirkly gone,
  As fast as he can win;
But before he came there, as we do hear,
  He was taken very ill.

罗宾汉之死

1

话说罗宾汉与小约翰，

　　当啷当啷当啷啷，

一道走在鲜花盛开的堤岸。

　　勇敢的罗宾对小约翰说：

"我们射过箭成千累万。"

　　嘿，当啷当啷当啷啷！

2

"如今我却拉不开弓，

　　长箭不能凌空飞翔。

山下住着我的堂姐，

　　她会为我把瘀血放一放。"

3

罗宾汉匆匆忙忙上路，

　　赶往美丽的克考里寺院。

听说他在出发以前，

　　已经生过一场重病。

4

And when he came to fair Kirkly-hall,

    He knockd all at the ring,

But none was so ready as his cousin herself

    For to let bold Robin in.

5

"Will you please to sit down, cousin Rohin," she said,

    "And drink some beer with me?"

"No, I will neither eat nor drink,

    Till I am blooded by thee."

6

"Well, I have a room, cousin Robin," she said,

    "Which you did never see,

And if you please to walk therein,

    You blooded by me shall be."

7

She took him by the lily-white hand,

    And led him to a private room,

And there she blooded bold Robin Hood,

    While one drop of blood would run down.

8

She blooded him in a vein of the arm,

4

他来到美丽的克考里寺院，
　　使劲将门环敲响。
堂姐本人从屋里出来，
　　招呼勇敢的罗宾进房。

5

"请坐，罗宾堂弟，"她说，
　　"同我喝杯酒怎么样？"
"不必了，我不思饮食，
　　只求你将瘀血放一放。"

6

"好吧，罗宾汉堂弟，"她说，
　　"我有间私房你未见过；
如果你乐意到那里去，
　　我马上就给你放血。"

7

她用百合般雪白的手，
　　领他进入一间密室。
她要在那里为他放血，
　　鲜血将从罗宾身上流出。

8

她刺开他手上血管，

And locked him up in the room;

Then did he bleed all the live-long day,

Until the next day at noon.

9

He then bethought him of a casement there,

Thinking for to get down;

But was so weak he could not leap,

He could not get him down.

10

He then bethought him of his bugle-horn,

Which hung low down to his knee;

He set his horn unto his mouth,

And blew out weak blasts three.

11

Then Little John, when hearing him,

As he sat under a tree,

"I fear my master is now near dead,

He blows so wearily."

12

Then Little John to fair Kirkly is gone,

As fast as he ean dree;

But when he came to Kirkly-hall,

然后把他反锁在房。
他流了整整一天的血，
　　直流到第二天晌午。

9

当时他想爬起身，
　　去把房里窗户打开，
但已虚弱得动弹不得，
　　无法从床上下来。

10

他想起自己的号角，
　　那号角就挂在膝盖上。
他将号角移到嘴边，
　　吹出三阵低微的声响。

11

小约翰坐在一棵大树下，
　　听见罗宾汉的号角声。
"我的头领吹得多疲惫，
　　我担忧他生命垂危。"

12

小约翰火速起程，
　　赶往美丽的克考里。
他很快来到寺院，

He broke locks two or three:

13

Until he came bold Robin to see,
   Then he fell on his knee;
"A boon, a boon," cries Little John,
   "Master, I beg of thee."

14

"What is that boon," said Robin Hood,
   "Little John, [thou] begs of me?"
"It is to burn fair Kirkly-hall,
   And all their nunnery."

15

"Now nay, now nay," quoth Robin Hood,
   "That boon I'll not grant thee;
I never hurt woman in all my life,
   Nor men in woman's company.

16

"I never hurt fair maid in all my time,
   Nor at mine end shall it be;
But give me my bent bow in my hand,
   And a broad arrow I'll let flee
And where this arrow is taken up,

把几道门一一砸开。

13

他见到勇敢的罗宾汉，

　　上前恭敬地鞠躬行礼。

"我请求，我请求，"小约翰说，

　　"头领，我有一事请求。"

14

"什么请求？"罗宾汉问，

　　"小约翰，你有什么请求？"

"我请求火烧克考里，

　　烧掉她们的修道院。"

15

"不行，这可不行，"罗宾汉说，

　　"这请求我无法答应；

我一生从没伤害过妇女，

　　只要她们在场，男人也幸免。

16

"我一生从没伤害过姑娘，

　　临终时破规矩更不应当。

请把弯弓放到我手上，

　　我要让箭凌空飞翔。

这箭落在什么地方，

There shall my grave digged be.

17

"Lay me a green sod under my head,
    And another at my feet;
And lay my bent bow by my side,
    Which was my music sweet;
And make my grave of gravel and green,
    Which is most right and meet.

18

"Let me have length and breadth enough,
    With a green sod under my head;
That they may say, when I am dead,
    Here lies bold Robin Hood."

19

These words they readily granted him,
    Which did bold Robin please:
And there they huried bold Robin Hood,
    Within the fair Kirkleys.

那里就是我的坟场。

17

"请在我头上垫一片草皮，
　　再在我脚后也垫一片草皮。
我身边要搁上弯弓与锐箭，
　　那是我最心爱的乐音；
砾石与草皮随处都有，
　　正好用来筑我的坟茔。

18

"头枕着青青草皮，
　　让我舒服地在地下长眠。
我死后人们会这样说，
　　这里躺着勇敢的罗宾。"

19

他们满口答应他的请求，
　　勇敢的罗宾十分满意。
他们在那里将他掩埋，
　　坟墓就在美丽的克考里。

COMMENTS/注释

[1] 小约翰,罗宾汉的重要助手。

[2] 原来名字为John Little,改名后叫Little John。

[3] 诺贝,古代英国货币。

[4] 巴恩斯代尔,地名,在诺丁汉一带,当时被列为皇家猎园。

[5] 马克,旧时欧洲大陆的金银重量单位,一马克相当于八盎司。

[6] 在中世纪英国,政府要处决某个犯人,起用的刽子手一般由乞丐、流浪汉一类人。

[7] 理查一世(1157—1199),英国安茹王朝第二代国王,在位期间为1189—1199年。他是亨利二世第二个儿子。